How I Got Over
The Journey to Emancipation

Perry Malone

Copyright © 2012 by Perry Malone

How I Got Over
The Journey to Emancipation
by Perry Malone

Printed in the United States of America

ISBN 9781622303748

All rights reserved solely by the author. The author guarantees all contents are original and do not infringe upon the legal rights of any other person or work. No part of this book may be reproduced in any form without the permission of the author. The views expressed in this book are not necessarily those of the publisher.

Bible quotations are taken from the King James Version of the Bible.

www.xulonpress.com

Proverbs 15:3

The eyes of the Lord
are in every place,
beholding the evil
and the good.

Acknowledgements

I would like to thank my grandparents, Madear and Daddy, for loving me from birth, for raising me as their own, and always being there for me. Even though you've both gone home to be with the Lord, your memory and labor of love lives on in and through me. Love you, Baby! Love you Daddy!

I'd also like to thank Brother Gerald Brabham for his continuous encouragement, and for his stamp of approval concerning this book. You are a mighty man of valor and faithful servant to the Most High God. I'll see you on the outside, brother.

Thank you, Brother Harold Thompson, for being obedient to the Lord by telling me the revelation that was given to you for me to write this book. You are a true brother and friend. See you soon.

Thanks to my children for all that you've endured as well as contributed during this lengthy process. To my three princesses starting with the youngest, Kiara, Salena, and Jannae. To the one and only prince, Christopher. I love you all so much, and I'm so proud of how well you all have done while I was away. It's now time to start living. Are you with me? Thanks also for allowing me to help someone at the expense of our issues. We'll get it right in Part 2. Love you!

Thanks to my best friend, my spiritual sister, and greatest asset as it pertains to my spiritual maturity in the Lord. Love you, Sister Rosie.

I would like to acknowledge my beloved brother in the Lord, James Holmes, who has been in company with me for about ten years now. I've been to three institutions, and you've unintentionally followed me to each one. It was just recently that I had begun to see a level of growth concerning your spiritual maturity, which lead me to believe that you were on the right path to not only seeking out and finding your ordained purpose in the Lord, but preparing yourself for it, that our God may begin to strategize your plan of release.

I love you, my brother, and look forward to seeing you beyond these walls, prayerfully as a mature man of God with purpose. If not, then I look forward to hearing from you beyond these walls. So you had better redeem the time.

A special thanks to Brother Mike Felder for allowing me to sow into his life words of wisdom, and for having a zeal for the Lord to grow and to be used by Him. Love you, man.

Brother Willie Norton, thanks for being a sounding board, and for just being spiritually rugged, giving me no choice but to toughen up. Also for enduring my snoring all those nights. Love you, man.

To my loving mother, Christine. It's about to get much better, my gal. You mean the world to me, and I'm so sorry for all of the stress and the burden that I placed upon you by coming here. Never again! Love you.

To my sister, Rochelle. I love you and look forward to us doing big things together. Thanks for everything. Love you.

To all of my loving aunts: Lettie, Nancy, Arlene, Marshalla, and Maxine. You all have contributed in some way in being an asset to me or to this worthy cause, whether small or great. I thank you.

To Jimmy, Clinton, Abraham, George, Henry, Floyd, Mike, Charlie, Manly boy, Mendi Sue, Strudy, Tabitha, Marcus, Nia, Kristie, and everyone else who I may have forgotten. Please charge it to my head and not my heart. Love you.

To Mrs. Doris Lewis, my guardian angel. Thank you so much for your life of service and labor of love that you've extended towards me through all that you've invested in Jannae. Love you so much.

To the mothers of my children, Ramona, Prinstine, and Kate. Thank you all for carrying the load all these years. Love you!

I would like to thank and acknowledge these people of standard, who had faith enough in this project, so much so that they made a contribution with the belief that their return would be rewarding: Steven B. Speal, Reinaldo Echevarria Gomez, Jimmy Salcedo, Adair Johnson, D.A. Walker Young, and Keonya Adams. Love you!

I'd like to thank my brother and friend, Mr. B., for his contributions. Love you, man!

I would like to thank and honor a few true servants of the Most High God: Dr. Cox, our very own pastor here at FCI Jesup, for

Acknowledgements

ministering God's Word to His people week in and week out with the intent of building character and stability in men before leaving prison, that their chance of returning would be highly unlikely. Also Pastor Stanley Carter, Pastor Sellers and Brother Kicklighter, Reverend Lewis Goodwill and Mrs. Goodwill, and last but not least Pastor Joseph Wilkins. Thank you all for your unwavering sacrifice that you've made throughout the years for visiting God's people in prison. You all have truly made an impact in my life as well as many other brothers behind these prison walls that you've consistently sowed into their lives. May the Lord richly bless you for your labor of love.

Last but certainly not least, I'd like to thank my God, who's responsible for every word, thought, resource, ability, and increase concerning this divine project. I love You, Lord!

Chron. 16:9

Introduction

Some view coming to prison as a bad thing, but what if it had potentially saved your very life? There have been numerous times in my life while dealing in criminal activities where I found myself looking down the barrel of a gun. Although faced with life-threatening predicaments, none of which were persuasive enough to lead me into choosing a different way of life. Prison not only afforded me the opportunity of being isolated from that particular lifestyle long enough to realize just how foolish I had become, but it was also where I found the Lord, which ultimately changed my life forever.

Accompanied with the Lord saving me, He also extended His mercy towards me by unveiling a major government corruption scandal in my case as an attempt to frame me for capital murder. God gave me the evidence to prove it, which will lead to my deliverance. But while in prison, the Lord inspired me to write this book, which will not only expose just how far the government is willing to go in order to unlawfully obtain a conviction, but He has also graced me with the wisdom that has enabled me to teach simple truths through life experiences concerning family matters, the life of a prisoner, the life of a believer, and most importantly, understanding how to get God's attention, finding your purpose, and receiving the Lord's favor on your life.

The very thing that God has done for me, He's willing to do the same for you. I look forward to hearing from you regarding the impact this book has made in your life. Godspeed!

—Perry Malone

Contents

1 Anticipated Nightmare	**17**
Back in the Saddle	19
A Call to Salvation in Adversity	20
Who Is Above the Law?	21
2 A Reaffirmed Salvation in Adversity	**22**
Back in Population with a New Agenda	25
My Day in Court	26
Back to the Wedge on Eagle's Wings	27
Knocked Off My High Horse	27
3 Preparing to Face the Unknown	**29**
The Lord Met Me There with a Hug from an Old Friend	30
What Are They Up to Now?	32
At It Again, or Could Things Be Looking Up?	33
4 If Not Now, When Lord?	**36**
Diesel Therapy	37
The Real Big House	38
Not While in Prison	39
5 I'm Ready to Go	**42**
Final Destination Before Going Home	43
A Meeting with Destiny	44
Denominations Clash	46
Being Called into the Ministry	48
6 A Friend Who Became My Enemy Is My Friend	**51**
7 Looking for a Sign	**58**
Show Me the Money	60
A Get-Out-of-Jail-Free Card, Only It's Not Free	62

8 Family Crisis 65
   Tried Faith 67
   Watch Them Foxes 68
   A Father's Day Visit 71
   Children Never Outgrow Their Fathers 73
   Is There a Balm in Jesup? 74
   A Birthday Prayer for My Ex 76

9 Satan's Attempt to Steal God's Glory 78
   In Love with the Anointing 79
   The Life of a Song 80
   Another Family Crisis 81
   I Nearly Lost Him 83
   Trying to Get the Speck Out of Her Eye, I Discovered
   a Plank in Mine 84
   A Quest to Prepare an Unprepared Family for Wealth 86
   He Keeps Doing Great Things for Me 87

**10 Feeling Good About Knowing That Something Is About
    to Happen While Preparing for the Same 89**
   Should Christians Cooperate with the Government
   for the Purpose of a Sentence Reduction? 91
   Seize Every Moment Given by Your Children to Tell
   Them About God's Goodness and Their Need for Him 93
   Did God Make Us This Way? 95
   Who's the Mother? 96
   My Sister's Response 97

11 Twelve Days Before Christmas, 2010 99
   Identifying the Marks for the Making of God's Set Man 100
   Suicide Watch 102
   Unaltered Faith 103
   The Will to Live 104
   I Give 105
   He's with the Lord Now 107

Contents

12 Last Letter to Family Before Coming Home 109
    Town News 111
    Affirmation of Oneness 113
    Beware of Idols 115
    Unforgiveness 116
    In Response to Last Letter Before Coming Home ... 117

13 When Faith Fails, Trust 119
    I Don't Want to Miss God In This 120
    Rosie's Birthday 121
    My Birthday 123
    A Family Reunion 125
    Remembering Daddy on His Birthday 126

14 Should Christians Have the Liberty to Engage in Explicit Sexual Practices with Their Spouse Such as Oral Sex? 128
    My Babies Are Having Babies 131
    Suicide Watch Again? 134

15 It's for Her Good Also That I Not Be Named Amongst Those of a Bad Report 138
    That Which I Had Failed to Do 140
    An Emotional Father's Day 142
    Remembering the Reason for Writing 144
    Double Trouble 145
    Concluding the Matter 150

16 The Desire to Be Rich 151
    Is Anyone Prepared to Die? 153
    Testimonies 154
    11-11-11 / Remembering a Vet 157
    Merry Christmas, 2011 158

    More About the Project 161
    Attention Reader 163

1
Anticipated Nightmare

Here I am coming off the interstate headed back into Mobile on the passenger side of my cousin's car. It's very hot and humid and the windows are rolled down because there's no air conditioning in the car. But that's just the beginning of a nightmare that's becoming a living reality. I've just been informed by my attorney that the government wants to indict me in an ongoing drug conspiracy.

Days after receiving this information, it had gotten even worse. It was broadcasted on the news that the informant in this case had been murdered and I was wanted for questioning. So while getting off of the ramp, making it into Mobile, I noticed two familiar faces in the left lane of ongoing traffic from my peripheral. It was special agent Daryl Wallace and Anthony Cole. It was the two agents that had been looking for me. Wow! I felt like a helpless child on a roller coaster ride by himself for the very first time.

I sat still as a stone, thinking that if I were to blink, they'd notice. I didn't even let my cousin know that was driving, concerned that he might panic. So as we drove side by side for about a quarter of a mile, they turned left as their lips were moving. Undoubtedly their conversation was about how they would apprehend me. Little did they know, I was looking at them look for me.

What a predicament, I thought. If only I would have left town when my attorney, Ben Hernes, advised me to. But instead, I took the advice of my wife and stayed, knowing that she didn't have my best interest at heart. Her concern was for her mother, who was going through legal difficulties as well.

We both had been through so much together. Years of unfaithfulness and untrustworthiness left the both of us with nothing left to give. But emotional attachments wouldn't allow us to just let go.

Anyway, it's getting late, and I've been at my aunt's apartment for hours now, trying to figure out what's going on. I began to get thirsty, the kind of thirst that water nor soft drink could satisfy. So I asked my aunt if I could use her van to go to the liquor store. She threw me the keys and I left, headed up Airport Boulevard. I hadn't driven a quarter mile from my aunt's apartment before I noticed some colorful, flashing lights in my rearview mirror.

Oh my God, how I wished they were Christmas lights. But it wasn't the month of December, so that wish was immediately forced out of my mind. As my heart raced and my strength began to fail me, I turned my right signal light on to turn into the nearest parking lot, which happened to be the Warren Inn apartment complex. I immediately stopped the van and got out of it with my hands in the air to avoid them from later using their famous cliché, "We thought he had a gun."

As they approached me, I was handcuffed. Then I heard the voice of one agent as he came closer ask the question, "Is that him?" Once it was confirmed, another agent made eye contact with me and sarcastically said, "All dressed up with nowhere to go, huh?"

I was in the back seat of one agent's vehicle as we were racing down the highway as though we needed to reach our destination really fast. The only thing that was said to me on our way there was, "You are in a lot of trouble, and if I were you, I'd sing like a bird." I was so spaced out, it was as though he had said nothing at all. Within minutes we had arrived at a place that looked nothing like the Metro County Jail. It was the FBI headquarters. *Oh boy*, I thought, *this is gonna be a long night.*

So here I am in the interrogation room with Agent Cole, Agent Wallace, and the infamous Pete Barnes. "Perry, tell us what you know about the murder. We don't believe that you had anything to do with it, but we do believe that you know something about it," said Agent Cole. I immediately responded by saying that I knew nothing about any murder case. "Oh yes, you do, Perry. We know that nothing goes down without you knowing about it," said Pete Barnes.

After hours of being asked the same question but to no avail, Agent Wallace just lost it and shouted things to me that I dare not repeat. A long story short, he yelled, "If you don't tell us what we want to know, I'm gonna knock your head off with my pistol." At this point I'm shaking like Don Knotts. Refusing to make eye contact with him, I wondered if I'd make it out of there alive.

Then he drew closer, with his hand in the air as though he's about to strike me. As I held my breath, I heard a loud noise, but I felt no pain. My vision began to get blurry. Then I heard him say, "Look at her!" I looked down at the table, and it was a picture of a woman covered in blood that he had slammed on the table. This was obviously his informant that was murdered.

"Where is my attorney?" I asked for the third time.

"Ben Hernes can't help you; he's dying with cancer. Ha! Ha! Ha!" Cole exclaimed as he laughed. "Perry, you remember when I told you that I didn't need any evidence to put a drug case on you?" said Wallace vindictively. "Well, I'm gonna see to it that you get the death penalty for this murder if you don't tell us what you know."

Again I asked for my attorney. Finally they began to take me outside to be transported to the Metro County Jail. I never thought I'd be so relieved to go to jail. When I made it outside, I noticed a very familiar face being brought out as well. It was my wife. She had been interrogated as well. I called her name, and she angrily looked at me and answered, "What?" It was obvious that the agents had revealed to hear a few secrets of mine concerning women in order to try and get her to lie on me. I responded by saying, "Never mind," being persuaded that the emotional ties that had held us together for so long had finally been broken. I guess because of infidelity we've both been through that many times. But it was more convenient for her, being that I could be gone for a very long time.

Back in the Saddle

So here I am, back in the Metro County Jail. It's been a while, but nothing's changed: card playing, dominos, watching TV, talking on the telephone while holding one ear because of the loud noise, and fighting over food trays. After settling in and getting familiar with my surroundings, I decided to get in a card game. We were playing tunk for commissary. I wasn't doing so bad until I heard a news broadcast on the television that caught my attention. It was about the murder of the government witness that the government agent threatened me with. They were offering a large reward for any information leading to the arrest of the person responsible.

At this point I was charged with two bogus drug conspiracies that these agents put on me. *Framing me for a capital murder that I didn't do would be almost impossible*, I thought. Some time later I heard someone calling my name at the door. It was my cousin named Marcus, who we call Booney. He wanted to know if I was alright, and did I want him to move over in the wedge where I was. I told him no.

My cousin was always a problem child, and I had enough on my mind. His mother was my aunt. She's an evangelist. I don't know why ministers' children are usually like the devil's children. Maybe because ministers were devils' kids before they became ministers.

Days later I was sitting in my cell in deep thought about the trying times that were ahead when this tall CO, meaning "correctional officer," came to the door and began talking to me like he knew me. Well, he didn't really *know* me; he knew *of* me. Anyway, he wanted his car painted and he heard that I owned a paint and body shop on Houston Street and he was hoping that we could work something out. Well, at this time cigarettes were not allowed in the county jail, so he began to bring me some, along with food from the outside, like Church's and Popeye's chicken, etc. I started to sell cigarettes for fifty dollars a pack or five dollars for a single. I became the man of the wedge, well at least for a while.

A Call to Salvation in Adversity

One day I heard a familiar voice calling me to the door again. It was my cousin Booney. When I came to the door, he told me something that was so profound. Little did I know it would eventually change my life forever. He said, "Perry, my mama told me to tell you that you need to quit playing games and come on home." He then said, "I don't know what she meant by that, but she said that you would know." It had to be a divine word from God Himself. I didn't even have to ponder on it before concluding what I had perceived it to mean. How can a sinner like me know the voice of God when he hears it?

It was only a few days later that I flushed all the cigarettes down the toilet and began to get on my knees and cry out to God for salvation, although that didn't change my situation. Things began to get even worse. There was another broadcast on the news about the murder with a larger reward, but this time my name was mentioned as being the prime suspect. It wasn't long before my attorney told me that the government was conducting a grand jury to have me indicted for capital murder. I never felt so scared and helpless in all my life. *Where could they be getting this evidence from?* I thought. *I didn't kill anyone.*

Who Is Above the Law?

As I was going back and forth to court for pretrial hearings on the drug charges, I got a taste of just what the government can do. I thought that I was in a movie or a bad dream. I witnessed coercion, the prosecutor committing perjury, and the court reporter altering my transcripts in order to cover up their misconduct. This is too much for me; I've got to find a way out of here. From that day on I began to pay close attention to the U.S. Marshals as they punched in their code on the keypad that controlled the gate to let you in and out of the back entrance of the courthouse. It was obvious that this Christian thing wasn't helping at all. As a matter of fact, things had gotten worse.

By this time I had gone through several lawyers. It had become apparent that even they were controlled by and subject to the power of the government. I had concluded the obvious—the government was above the law.

Days later, I was told to pack it up. I was being moved to solitary confinement. The government told the warden to put me in the hole with several inmates that had brutally beaten and killed a man in that very wedge only a week ago. I was also stripped of all my privileges such as phone calls, visitation, religious services, commissary, recreation, etc., without a cause. They told the warden to lie and say that the U.S. Marshals had put me there for security purposes. This was all done in order to further their endeavor to frame me for capital murder of a government witness.

2
A Reaffirmed Salvation in Adversity

The pressure on me had become so intense that I had begun having nightmares and waking up in the middle of the night with panic attacks. At this point, I knew that I needed God more than ever; and if I was going to make it through this, He was going to have to supernaturally intervene. So then and there, I got back on my knees and cried out to the Lord. This time, to my surprise, I didn't ask Him to deliver me out of my situation, but to give me the strength to make it through it.

At that moment a peace came upon me that passes all understanding. I was given a desire to want to spend every waking moment studying the Word of God and talking with Him in prayer. It wasn't long before He began creating opportunities for me to witness to others in the surrounding holding cells, including the men that had recently killed a man in there for making too much noise.

Soon they had begun opening up to me about things they had heard concerning the government's attempt to frame me for capital murder. They had revealed to me the names of certain individuals that had been or were going to the grand jury to testify of things that they heard me say or directly told them specific details about the murder. I told them that I hadn't so much as heard of those names before. They responded by saying they believed me, and that they would be willing to allow my attorney to come and interview them.

What a sigh of relief, I thought, while trying to suppress my true feelings. I began to wonder if what they heard would be enough to save my life. After all, I've witnessed firsthand just how corrupt the government is with no one to answer to but themselves.

As I was going back and forth to trial on the two drug conspiracy charges, I was denied the right to present evidence and testimony to the jury that would have acquitted me. For some reason, I was not that surprised. I understood that making sure I got convicted would better their chances of getting me the death penalty in the capital murder case.

After being found guilty and looking at two mandatory life sentences, I still managed to stay focused. And while my family was drenched with tears, I boldly made it known to the court that I was aware that the government had taken the position of framing me for capital murder. I also stated that my attorney was aware of this ongoing conspiracy to violate my rights.

After putting them all on the spot, the judge told my attorney that if he found these allegations to have some truth to them, then he should report it to the attorney general's office. Although reluctant, he eventually did just that. Amazingly, that didn't slow the government down—not one bit. But the more they tried to destroy me, the stronger I became. And to think someone once said this Christian stuff didn't work! Thank God I didn't listen to the voice of doubt. Surely I would have lost my mind by now.

Days later while I was in my cell witnessing to a young man through the vent, another inmate called my name and asked me how I was doing, as though he knew me. I responded by saying, "I'm truly blessed." He went on to say that I didn't know him, and that he wanted to warn me of the government's plan to frame me for capital murder. I asked him to tell me everything he knew about it, but he refused to do so out of fear. So I told him that I understood. I then thanked him and said that I would remember him in my prayers.

The very next morning he called my name with a very fearful tone of voice. I knew that something very important was sure to follow. After I responded, he began telling me in detail how he knew that the government was trying to frame me. He said that he was a part of this conspiracy against me. He went on to tell me everything that had happened.

One day he was in the federal courthouse holding cell after coming back from sentencing, feeling very emotional knowing that he was about to do years in prison for the very first time. A young man was brought in the cell with him that he never had seen before and asked the strangest question, "Do you wanna go home?"

Confused, he reluctantly responded by saying, "Yeah, I do." The young man began to tell him about a murder that took place.

He gave him the name of the victim, the time and place of the crime, the type of weapon that was used, and the name of the murderer, which supposedly was me. He gave him the name of the agents to call once he got back to his assigned cell, and instructed him to tell the agents that he had heard Perry Malone give this information to his codefendant. The agents would then come and interview him, give him a polygraph test that he would automatically pass, then allow him to take this fabricated and coerced evidence before the grand jury in order to get an indictment on me. Excited about going home, he immediately made the call to the agents once he made it back to his cell. They soon paid him a visit.

After confirming the fabricated details about the murder, he was eventually transferred back to the courthouse for the next phase of the plot—to take the predetermined lie detector test. But when he got there, something out of the ordinary happened. The spirit of fear, weakness, and self-preservation had left him. He began to have compassion on someone he had never met.

He told the agents that it was all a lie, and that he was coerced to do it in exchange for a sentence reduction. He went on to say that he just couldn't take an innocent man's life without a cause. He told them that he would be willing to wear a wire in order to help them catch the guy that coerced him. They weren't interested in that. Instead they tried to convince him that the information he provided was true, and that he should proceed with the process.

After repeatedly refusing to assist them in framing an innocent man for murder, the agent became furious and very belligerent, threatening to give him more time, and using language terms that one would speak while talking to a homosexual. True enough, he was given more time for giving false information to a government agent, even though the agent was the one that provided this false information to him through their informant.

Although he refused to continue in this unjust act, he told me that many others did. Their informant was being moved from wedge to wedge recruiting others that were interested in a time cut. If it had not been for the government vindictively putting me in the hole, and this young man getting in a fight being put in the hole next to me, I'd be on death row right now. Although this was some pretty staggering news, I took comfort in the fact that God sent someone to help me.

After receiving a visit from my attorney and sharing with him what was revealed to me, I urged him to come and interview this young man so that I could have this information documented before they transported him to prison. It was only a couple of days before they shipped him away.

I began to think that my attorney notified the government concerning this witness; therefore they had him moved immediately. I didn't really know what God was doing at the time, but I refused to believe that meeting this young man was coincidental and that this information was lost forever.

Back in Population with a New Agenda

Not long after, I was moved back to population, but for some reason they put me in the wedge next to my original one. As I passed by my old wedge, some of the guys that were in there with me gave a hard and unfriendly stare that made it obvious that they no longer saw me in the same light as before.

Once I got situated in my new cell, it was revealed to me that the government informant had been in my old wedge, even in the very cell that I was assigned to. That explained the unfriendly stares I received on my way over there. So it was official; everyone believed me to be a murderer, and I had become a get-out-of-jail-free pass. Still nothing stood in my way of studying God's Word and growing in the faith.

Shortly after, I started a Bible study with men that wanted God to intervene in their situation more than anything. There's something about going to jail and facing serious prison time that makes the average person call upon the name of the Lord. For the most part we just want to be delivered from prison and not from our sins. So just as we tried to manipulate the system, we think that we can actually manipulate an omniscient God.

Even thought the study was going well, I had only been a Christian for about eight months. I was a bit overzealous, and not as mature as one should be when it comes to teaching the Word of God, although the Lord did teach me a lot during that eight-month period that I was able to impart to the young converts. I believe that the patience I was given to listen to their problems, and although I was facing a mandatory life sentence, still being able to encourage and uplift them gave many the strength to move forward.

Soon the time had arrived for me to go back to court for sentencing. The brothers encouraged me, and figured that there was no way God would allow the judge to give me a life sentence. I knew differently. God not only allows those He loves to go through various trials for His glory, but He also equips and prepares them for it. To God be the glory! I was ready to be used by Him.

My Day in Court

So here I am, in front of the judge, and he posed the question: "Do you have anything that you would like to say before sentencing?" I emphatically responded with a "Yes!" I began by reiterating the fact that the prosecutor as well as the government agents had gone through extreme measures to violate my rights by not only committing perjury, falsifying documents, and altering my pretrial hearing transcripts, but they had also conspired to unjustly take my very life by attempting to frame me for a capital murder.

I went on to tell the judge that he had knowledge of these unjust acts, but failed to review the evidence that was available. I then told him that because of his foreknowledge of this crime and his failure to intervene, he was as guilty as the government. Furthermore, I would not ask this court for mercy, because this justice system doesn't possess such a quality, but the God that I serve does, and He has the final word.

The courtroom was filled with news reporters due to the nature of my case being the first potential federal capital murder case in Mobile. The judge began to respond before knowing what to say. Once he gathered his composure, he began to defend himself by giving a lifelong devotion of upholding the law speech. After it was over, he sentenced me to life in prison. I then looked back at my family to extend words of encouragement, then was taken out of the courtroom to be transferred back to my cell.

Back to the Wedge on Eagle's Wings

As I walked in the wedge, it was as though the peace of God was carrying me. I had a smile on my face that led many to believe I was going home. My Christian brothers followed me into my cell to hear a testimony that they thought would prove to be anything other than a life sentence.

As I was giving them the details about what had happened, they began to be saddened by the fact that I might not ever get out of prison. But I endeavored to build them up on their most holy faith, that they may see through the eyes of God and share the same hope as I did of reuniting with my family again. My desire was that they would rejoice with me over the fact that in the face of fear and adversity, while being given a life sentence, the joy of the Lord was my strength.

Although I hadn't been in the Lord for very long, I realized that I was in the midst of babes in Christ; and it was only by the mercy of God that I had been extended such divine grace to endure these trying times, yet with faith of a better tomorrow.

Knocked Off My High Horse

A few days had gone by, and my name was called for a visit. *Who could it be?* I thought to myself as I drew closer to the visiting room. As I approached the booth, to my surprise, it was my wife! I hadn't seen or spoken to her in months due to solitary confinement. So I picked up the phone and we began to talk.

She seemed to be doing really well under the circumstances. Once we had gotten past the small talk, she told me that she and the kids went fishing. I initially found that to be funny, being that she never liked fishing. To prolong the humor, I asked who they went with. Her response was, her boyfriend. Remind you, I had just been sentenced to life in prison only a few days prior to this visit, and I handled it very well, to God be the glory. But this, I just wasn't ready for.

As my heart began to fail me, I found myself falling off my spiritual high horse. *Why does this hurt so bad?* I thought. She had cheated on me several times in the past while I was out there with her, as did I. Maybe it was because I thought she wanted to hurt me on purpose, and the fact that she was pretty heartless to do it at a time like this. Or was it those emotional attachments that I failed to deal with that had come back to haunt me?

Pretending to be unaffected by the news, with a straight face I asked a meaningless question, "How long have you been seeing him?" She responded by saying I must have known that she'd be seeing someone by now. As my mind began to drift, I started visualizing this unknown man being a father to my children. I think that must have hurt the most.

As the time winded down and I heard the CO holler, "Visitation over," I ended it by saying, "When we get our divorce and you marry him, I hope that the two of you will be happy." She then said, when I came home we'd get back together. I just nodded my head to express to her that I totally disagreed.

After saying good-bye, I staggered out of there as though I had just come out of a gas chamber. "Well, Lord," I said, "I sure do hope that You've got some more of that grace, because I'm fresh out." As I approached the wedge door, I knew that I had to at least look as though nothing was wrong, for my younger brothers. But I knew that the eyes were the key to the soul, and if I was to make eye contact with anyone, I would have some explaining to do, when all that I really wanted to do was make it to my cell and put up the "Do Not Disturb" blanket and talk to the Lord.

Once the CO buzzed me in, I moved swiftly to my cell as though I needed to use the bathroom. So I made it in there with no problem; not to mention, my cellie was in the day room watching television. The Lord must have prepared the way. He knew that we needed to talk.

After I had put the blanket up and began to commune with the Lord, I sensed Him saying to me, "I'm all you need. My grace is sufficient for you, for My strength is made perfect in weakness." I was comforted by the peace and love of God. What an awesome God!

3
Preparing to Face the Unknown

In the days to come, I knew that I had to get spiritually prepared to go to a place that I had never been before—a United States penitentiary. I really didn't know what to expect, other than the fact that the Lord would be with me. If He was in the fire with the three Hebrew boys, then surely He would be with me in the furnace of affliction. Daily I studied His Word and spent time with the brethren, getting prepared, as well as preparing them for my departure.

It wasn't many days after when I was awakened at about 2:00 a.m. by the CO with those grievous words: "Pack it up; you're catching the chain." It was almost like when someone wakes you up out of your sleep to tell you that you just lost a loved one. As I got myself together and said farewell to my Christian brothers, I started out the door on the journey of my life. Even though I didn't feel the presence of the Lord with me, I refused to believe that He wasn't.

While I was waiting on the U.S. Marshals in that cold holding cell, I began to read my small pocket Bible, reassuring me that He will never leave nor forsake me. Soon I began to hear the clinking sound of handcuffs and leg irons. I thought about the vow that I had made to myself how I'd never get on an airplane. I'd give almost anything not to break it right now.

When it became my turn to get shackled down, I was given an extra gadget due to the life sentence that I had—a little black box to go around my wrist in order to keep me from moving them, as though I was some kind of mass murderer. And to think I hadn't even made it to prison yet. I got the feeling that I was in for the ride of my life, and now facing what was my biggest fear, flying on an airplane, is just the tip of the iceberg.

Once we made it to the airplane and began to take off, in no time at all we were up in the clouds. Suddenly the fear of flying that I've had for so long was justified. It turns out that it was much worse than I had imagined. There were more bumps in the sky than on a dirt road in the country. I was certain that this was something I could never get use to.

Finally we made it to Oklahoma Transfer Facility where I met a man for the first time that was named in my indictment. He later told me that he was also a victim to Agent Wallace's unlawful interrogation tactics. Once he gave me the details, it sounded almost exactly like the encounter that I had with him on the night of my arrest. *How could someone who seemed to be a racist as well as a loose cannon work for law enforcement for so long without being reprimanded?* I thought. We didn't talk for very long before we were both transferred to different locations.

The Lord Met Me There with a Hug from an Old Friend

I later arrived at my destination, which was in Edgefield, South Carolina. It seemed to be a fairly peaceful prison. Five minutes after hitting the compound while walking with someone that I had just met, we were both threatened by a complete stranger who claimed we were walking too close to him. He was very belligerent, and it was obvious that he was mentally challenged. I don't know if his intentions were to scare us or what. If that was the case, he could've taken a bow, because he had far exceeded his expectations.

I encouraged Naughty, the young man I was walking with, to keep going. I refused to believe that things were as bad as they seemed. I began to understand how God allows those whom He loves to go through various trials in order to bring them to a place where they can be used by Him for His glory.

Not long after, the Lord revealed to me His purpose for me coming to Edgefield, South Carolina. One evening I was in the chow hall eating dinner when I saw a familiar face, as if it were the face of an angel. It was Wesley Bell, the young man that I had met in the lockup in the Metro County Jail. He was the one that God had changed his mind in assisting the government in trying to frame me for the capital murder. But he was taken out and sent to prison before I had the chance to have him interviewed. I could do nothing but run to him and hug him as though I'd known him all my life. I was consumed with joy because of the goodness of God. I knew that the Lord had brought him here to save my life.

Once I finally settled down, I asked him what he was doing here. He told me that he was at Atlanta U.S. Penitentiary and had gotten into a fight, so he was sent here. Now remind you, this was the same reason why he was put in solitary confinement right next to me at the Metro County Jail. Undoubtedly the Lord was revealing to me His power and presence in my life so that my faith would be increased. Little did I know I would be locked up longer than I expected; therefore His confirmation that I wasn't alone was well needed.

Anyway, Bell and I talked often to one another, reliving the past events that we both went through while under the merciless authority of certain government officials. No one would believe that the government is corrupt unless they had witnessed it for themselves. At least I didn't.

Bell wrote a sworn affidavit and had it notarized for me concerning the government's plot to take my life. *It still all seemed like one big nightmare to me, but when would it end?* I thought.

The institution turned out to be a fairly decent prison, especially compared to the Metro County Jail. The food was much better, and so were the religious services. Some of the Christian brothers there were far more mature than I was in the Word. Therefore I was looking forward to growing in the Lord.

Occasionally I called home to see how my family was doing and to hear that the government was still trying to pin the murder on me. I was told by Eric Curry, who used to be the mechanic at my paint and body shop, that the agents offered him a large sum of money to testify that I murdered a government witness and gave him the murder weapon to throw in a river, but he refused. I knew that the Lord was with me, and that He was greater than my enemies. But at times I felt like a sheep headed to the slaughter.

Neither my family nor I had the money to hire an attorney without fear of the government and the integrity to use this evidence in hopes that it would set me free. The problem was that it would not only set me free, but it would also bring about a criminal investigation on the government.

What Are They Up to Now?

Finally I decided to file a civil suit on my own, naming nine government employees for conspiring to take away my freedom and to frame me for a capital murder. I knew very little about filing legal documents in federal court, so filing against the government in their court would obviously be an uphill battle, to say the least.

Once I got started, I received a letter in the mail from the courts notifying me that I would be coming back there to prove where the money came from to hire my attorney. Being that I was appointed an attorney at trial, where did I get five thousand dollars from to hire one for my appeal? That made very little sense being that I had already told the judge at sentencing that my family was planning to hire an attorney for my appeal. So it was apparent to me that they had ulterior motives.

When I had made it back to Mobile, there were about six inmates in the van. Once we had arrived at the Metro County Jail, everyone got out except for me. For some reason the marshals were taking me to a different holding facility. About twenty minutes later, we were pulling up in Daphne, Alabama. It was a city jail for misdemeanors. The marshals were so kind to me. They laughed and joked with me all the way there.

I had never been to a jail with so much freedom. I had my own room for the majority of the time I was there. The phone was right by my cell. In addition to the jail phone, they also had a pay phone next to it. Your relatives were able to visit you and bring you money. As strange as it may seem, the outside door was right next to the visiting room. I was able to go outside for recreation alone, without other inmates or COs, and the fence was very short.

One or two correctional officers worked there at a time and they were normally women. It was right off the highway, and the COs' parking place was right in front of the little recreational cage where I would play basketball. I would see them pull up often, and sometimes they wouldn't even turn their ignition off. They would run in for a few minutes and come back out and leave. And to top it all off, the food was catered by my ex-girlfriend and her mother! It was like paradise in prison, or so I thought.

After my court hearing was over and my family had reiterated to the court where the money came from to hire an attorney for my appeal, I stayed in Daphne City Jail for at least another six weeks before I had my family call the Marshals' office to find out why I hadn't been transferred back to Edgefield, South Carolina. Don't get me wrong; I wanted to stay there until the Lord brought me home. I knew that I had it better than anyone in my position could ever ask for, but that was the problem.

I was persuaded that I was brought here for a reason: to attempt an escape, to either be killed, or to look guilty of capital murder. There was no other reason why a maximum-security prisoner with a life sentence would be brought to a misdemeanor jail with the liberty that I was given. The government was very crafty and cunning, like someone I know. But again, the wisdom of God had prevailed.

Finally, the marshals came to take me back to prison. They were the same ones that brought me here, but they were no longer friendly. It was like I had become their worst enemy, but why? I wonder if I would've taken the bait and tried to escape, would we still be friends? Yeah, right.

Once I made it back to Edgefield, some of the guys there had doubts as to why I really went back to court. That's the norm in prison; any time someone goes back to court, it's to testify against someone for a time-out. So for a while I was looked at kind of funny, but it soon blew over. I had soon gotten back into the flow of things, and it was as if I had never left.

At It Again, or Could Things Be Looking Up?

Then just like that, the government was at it again. I got locked up in the SHU, meaning Special Housing Unit, for no reason. I wondered if it was because of the lawsuit that I had begun filing, and maybe they were trying to make me miss the two-year statute of limitations deadline.

But after about a week I received a visit from two federal agents out of South Carolina. They said that they had received information that one of my codefendants that I met for the first time in Oklahoma Holding Facility told me that he was going to kill Agent

Daryl Wallace once he got out. They said that the district attorney was prepared to give me a time cut if I would make a statement against him.

This didn't make any sense to me. I knew that there was something else to this picture, but I couldn't put my hands on it. The government was trying to get me the death penalty. Why would they want to give me a time cut? Besides that, it was a lie, and I refuse to do anyone the way I've been done.

They spent about an hour trying to convince me to change my mind. After repeatedly refusing to make false statements against this innocent man, they left. Within the next couple of days I was released back onto the compound.

Of course the incident brought about more suspicion of whether or not I was trying to get a time cut. What had just happened didn't make much sense to me, so how could I expect for it to make sense to anyone that I told? It seemed as though the government was trying to put as much pressure on me as possible in order to force me into confessing to them who actually murdered their informant—something I knew nothing about.

But they were adamant about it, and they would stop at nothing to make sure that someone took the fall—not because they cared about the death of their informant, but because Agent Wallace failed in taking the necessary precautions of protecting her. Therefore his career was on the line, and the only thing that could save it was to solve the murder, or in his case, find someone to take the fall. Soon enough, it became apparent why the government wanted to give me a time cut if I were to lie on one of my codefendants.

Less than a week later, I was called up front for a visit. To my surprise, it was two agents out of Washington, DC. They were assigned to investigate the allegations that were made by my Aunt Louise on my behalf regarding Agent Daryl Wallace and his unlawful interrogation tactics that were used on me the night of my arrest. My aunt was the vice president of the NAACP of the Mobile branch at the time before she became the president.

They weren't very concerned about the government trying to frame me for murder, nor the prosecution perjury claims and the altering of my transcripts, things that could be easily proven by the evidence that was available. They chose to investigate the one claim that would be determined by whose testimony would be more credible—mine or the collaborated testimony of the agents that were in the room with us that night. The key question around the entire investigation was whether or not Agent Walton brandished his gun when he threatened to hit me in the head with it.

I volunteered to take a lie detector test. It was during that process when I had realized, in my opinion, that the government was corrupt not only on the local level, but all the way up to Washington, DC.

As I began to take the test, one of the agents instructed me on how it worked, and exactly what certain patterns meant. Once I was done taking the test, I was told that I had failed the part where I was asked if he brandished his gun. Out of disbelief, I asked if I could see the pattern sheet that showed I was lying. He reluctantly allowed me to see it. The test showed it was inconclusive.

After making that known to him, he began to get upset and snatched the pattern sheet from me. "Look!" he said. "Agent Wallace is already in trouble. Don't allow him to get punished for something that he didn't do!"

He asked me to recant my previous statement and say that he only threatened to use his pistol, but didn't brandish it. He also told me that if I didn't recant my statement, that the other allegations that were filed on my behalf wouldn't get investigated. One thing that I've learned about the government—they don't do too much bluffing. But I refused to lie by recanting my statement in order to help save the career of the agent who was trying to take my life.

So they left, and while the investigation was still pending, I mailed a copy of the evidence that supported my allegations to the agent in Washington, DC. I then called him to verify receiving the material. He denied ever getting it. So I decided to send it certified with a return receipt. Again, he denied receiving it, and said there were entirely too many employees working there for him to find out who the person was that signed for the package. He also stated that the investigation was just about over, and that there was not enough evidence to warrant a criminal prosecution on Agent Wallace.

4
If Not Now, When Lord?

Although it seemed all was lost and the government was above the law, I continued to trust in my God. There was no one else that could help me. Neither my family nor I had the money to hire an out-of-town attorney with the influence and stability to expose the unjust works of the government.

The attorney that we hired refused to bring up any issues that would challenge the government's misconduct. Not only did he do nothing to try and win my appeal, but after losing it, he tried to convince me to plead guilty to the murder, but to no avail. He then agreed to testify against me for the government once I had filed my prose habeas petition.

They made sure that they had done everything in their power to try and break me, in hopes that I would become vulnerable enough to not only lie on myself, but others as well.

Not long after my attorney, Arthur Daily, had betrayed me, he was elected Congressman of Alabama. It is my belief that it was the government's persuasion that put him in this position for his cooperation in their conspiracy against me.

I've got to tell you, I can't take any of the credit for not just giving up. God knows this was more than I could handle. But God just wouldn't let go of me. It was as though the Lord had turned me over to Satan to have his way with me. But just as He did Job, He forbids Satan to take my life. I'm also expecting to have a favorable and prosperous outcome as well, as did Job.

By now, I was a little paranoid and just unsure as to what the government would or would not do. The thought of them going as far as trying to have me killed even had crossed my mind. I began to have nightmares about the things that the government had put me through that resulted in me waking up in the middle of the night with no breath left in me. Each time it happened I found myself fighting for my life. Trying desperately to regain control of my breathing always seemed helpless, but somehow oxygen would eventually come from somewhere. I wanted to talk with medical or psychology about my problem, but I feared the government finding out about it, and somehow using it to their advantage.

Diesel Therapy

I had been in Edgefield for about a year now, and things seemed to be going alright. There wasn't much violence there, the food wasn't bad, and I had grown pretty close with some of the Christian brothers. I even befriended a few unbelievers at my workplace, hoping that they would be drawn to the Lord by my lifestyle.

All was well until one day I was called into the case manager's office only to find out that I was about to transfer to a real United States penitentiary. You would think by now that I would've become numb to bad news considering how frequently I would hear it, but not so. Now I was reminiscing about the things that I had heard that go on inside the pen. Of course, "pen" is a three-letter word that prisoners often use to mean penitentiary.

So being that I was already paranoid, I began to believe that there was nothing that the government wouldn't do to make sure that I would take the rap for this murder, even if it meant sending me to a penitentiary to have me killed, being that killing is the norm there. But the only thing that brought me comfort was the fact that I was still holding on to the Word that the Lord had spoken unto me. Therefore, I knew that no weapon formed against me would prosper.

So the time had come for me to transfer and once again face getting back on that big mechanical bird in the sky. It's amazing how the fear of that gave me a temporary case of amnesia as to my final destination, and having to face the unknown once I arrived.

So now I'm up in the air, excuse me, *way* up in the air, and I hear and feel some sputtering coming from the airplane. *I know we're not out of gas*, I thought to myself. Unfortunately we were, and had to make a pit stop to fuel up. Now I've run out of gas before in my car due to being in a hurry or just lazy, but this is *not* something that you do in the sky in an airplane! Boy, I tell you, this was enough to make a preacher cuss!

The Real Big House

So after going through holdovers and finally arriving at USP Pollock, surprisingly things appeared to be going well. I was one of the first few hundred there, and being that I was one of the first to open up the joint, it started out running smoothly.

We had single cells starting out, the food was great, and violence was at a minimum. But I had heard enough to know that I had better enjoy it while I could. What I didn't know was I was going to be there for over six years, and during that time span things would change dramatically.

So being that I wasn't the only one that came from Edgefield, SC, I was pretty familiar with some of the inmates that came with me. Although they were all in for violent crimes, they seemed to be pretty decent people. One of the guys who we called Blount (I'm assuming because he smoked a lot of marijuana), I could tell that he came from a good family and was raised right, but like most of us, just strayed away from what we knew to be right. Little did I know, this young man would affect my life in a major way some years down the road. But we'll get into that a little later.

Well, my weekly routine was simple. I went to church services as often as they would have them. There was limited Bible studying in the unit, in which I regret until this day. I watched television, institutional basketball games, I worked, and last but not least, I cooked myself a meal in the microwave whenever I didn't like what was being served in the chow hall.

Unfortunately, out of all these activities, cooking in the microwave consumed most of my time. I went from cooking for myself to eight or nine guys, until I eventually started selling food to the whole compound. I didn't like turning people down, and since I was investing a lot of time into it, I thought it wasn't robbery to get paid for my services.

I became really good at what I did, selling fried crust pizzas, hot pockets, nachos, gumbo, burrito pie, spaghetti, even country-style fish and grits. I was getting so much business until I had to hire a couple of guys to help me. This all sounds good from a worldly perspective, but I later came to realize that God was not pleased with it.

I was buying stolen items out of the kitchen; it took up my study time in the unit; when I went to church services, there were times when I couldn't even focus on what the preacher was saying for thinking about what I needed to do in order to prepare the meals I had to cook for my loyal customers. So basically I allowed the enemy to keep me busy enough to stop growing in God, which ultimately prolonged my stay in prison.

God promised to deliver me out of prison for His glory. But how much glory can God actually get from a Christian who's not prepared? There were times when the Lord had revealed this to me, and I attempted to retire from cooking. But my loyalty to my customers unknowingly outweighed and drowned out the voice of God.

At some point I met this strange man called Israel. He was either on his knees outside, looking up to the sky with his hands held up, with no socks, shoes, or shirt on, praying to his god. Other times he would just lie in the sun the same way, half dressed. To my surprise, we became real close. He was from my hometown, but his views about life and God were quite contrary to mine, which didn't come as a surprise.

He believed that the Messiah was a man who is currently walking the earth and had just been released from prison. He was so convinced that he made a statement that if this man would tell him to cut his children's heads off, he wouldn't hesitate to do it. I thought to myself, *Wow! Lord, I wish there was something I could do or say to help this guy.* Unfortunately, the six-and-a-half years that we were around one another, I couldn't.

Not While in Prison

Well, the time had come when I was about to face a moment in time that most of us face while being incarcerated for a significant amount of time. There I was, working in UNICOR, when my supervisor approached me and calmly told me that I was wanted in the chapel. *Oh no*, I thought to myself, *please don't let this be my grandmother passing.* She had been sick lately, but I was hoping that the Lord would see her through.

This wasn't just an ordinary grandmother. When I was born, they took me from the hospital straight to her house, where I remained until I moved out on my own. She and my grandfather raised me, fed me, and clothed me. When I went to jail, she was the one who put up her house to bail me out. Besides that, since I've been incarcerated, I can count the times that I actually called to check on her, and to let her know that I was OK, knowing that she often worried about me.

As I walked into the chaplain's office, he confirmed to me the very thing that I had feared: Madea had passed. He allowed me to make a phone call to my family. As he was dialing the number, I had to try and regain my composure. I had been encouraging my family ever since I got locked up that all was well and that I would be with them soon. So for them to see or hear me lose it was the last thing that they needed, especially at a time like this.

The phone began to ring, and my aunt said, "Hello," and as she began to talk about how my grandmother departed this life, tears began to flow and my voice began to betray me. I was grateful that she was one of the stronger ones in the family, although that didn't matter much, because afterwards she had told the whole family how I took it, and they were all up here to see about me the very next visiting day.

As we were all in the visiting room sharing and reminiscing about our Madea, the young man that I had spoken about earlier by the name of Blount was visiting with his family as well. He had gotten my attention and began to wave at me, along with an older lady whom I assumed was his aunt.

As we made eye contact, she had that familiar look that I've seen in the past when a female is attracted to you. But I didn't pay it any mind; I was kind of consumed with my present situation. Besides that, she was not my type.

After we had concluded our visit, I later saw Blount on the compound and he told me that his aunt liked me. Being that I wasn't interested, I kind of played it off with a nonchalant giggle, hoping that he wouldn't see through it. He later blurted out on several occasions that I was going to be his uncle. Although he did convince me to write and encourage her one day, being that she was going through something at the time, not to mention the fact that she was supposed to be a devout Christian, I felt that was the right thing to do. Her name was Rosie, but once she responded and told me that she was doing OK, I didn't see any reason to further correspond with her.

5
I'm Ready to Go

Well, I had been here at Pollock for some years now, and violence was at an all-time high. Men were getting stabbed and hit in the head with locks at least once a day. I never liked violence, and being that it had affected my cooking business, I disliked it even more.

Sometimes we would go on lockdown anywhere from a week to a month at a time. Oftentimes we would get off of lockdown just to go right back on it. In between those times, I would attempt to prepare the food for my illegal restaurant. Once I had spent about a hundred dollars on food supplies from the commissary as well as the kitchen, not to mention countless hours of preparations, we would go right back on lockdown. Knowing that the staff there was going to throw it all away during the shakedown, my only repeated response was to eat what I could and to throw away what I couldn't. That became really frustrating to the point that I wanted to retire more than ever. I began to think that the Lord was using this to convince me to stop.

People were getting killed on every hand, and the spirit of hatred, bitterness, and violence was so heavy in that place whereas you didn't have to be spiritual to sense it.

Every day the CO in the gun tower would drop what we call "bombs" on the yard that would shake the ground and scare the daylights out of you, in hopes of stopping a knife fight. It usually didn't stop the fight, but it did scare the daylights out of you. I guess one out of two ain't bad!

I became convinced that it was time to leave that place and get serious about God's business. So I cried out to God, that if He would deliver me from there, I would not only stop selling food, but

I would also become dedicated to getting prepared for the miracle that He had been wanting to manifest in my life for His glory.

The time had arrived for me to see my unit team and to possibly get put in for a transfer to go to a lower security prison. All went well. Now I had to wait for about a month to see whether or not I was approved.

During the waiting period, there were times when I didn't really want to transfer because I had grown very close to some of the guys there, especially my brothers in the Lord. I couldn't even find the nerve to tell them that I had been put in for a transfer until the day had finally come for me to pack out. I know that wasn't right, but I just couldn't stand to see the disappointment on their faces until it was absolutely necessary.

Once I packed out and exchanged information with my brothers on how to keep in contact with one another, I was off to my next journey.

Final Destination Before Going Home

After going through the torture of transferring and the airplane rides for the fourth time, I had reached my destination. I had heard a lot of comforting things concerning FCI (Federal Correctional Institution), Jesup, Georgia, especially the fact that you hardly even see a fistfight there.

As I walked on the compound, it resembled a college campus. That in itself took my expectation level up to an all-time high. Once I made it to my unit and got settled in, the very next thing was for me to get introduced to my Christian brothers.

One of the things that I had noticed about them right away was the fact that they were much more mature and dedicated to the Lord than the brothers that I had just left at Pollock USP. Although this wasn't one of the prison selections that I had told my unit team that I wanted to transfer to, I knew that this was where God had wanted me to be.

The Lord had brought me to a place where I had no excuse for not keeping the vow that I had made to Him. You know the one; that if He were to move me from that battlefield called Pollock, that I would stop selling food and get prepared for my release that He may get the glory that He so deserves.

Well, I must say, I started off pretty aggressively growing in the things of God. I began attending four Christian services a week, not to mention regularly fellowshipping with the brethren that were stronger than I was in the Lord. The more I was around them, the more it reminded me of all the years that I wasted being stagnant in the Lord, selling food and chasing stamps, which was the monetary currency on the compound at Pollock, as opposed to seizing every waking moment growing in God and seeking His purpose for my life.

I especially liked the Bible study in the unit, except for when one of the brothers would ask me to expound on the topic that we were discussing, or even to ask me to sing. I've always been nervous when it came to speaking or doing anything before a group of people, knowing that I was the center of attention. My hands would shake and my heart would beat so fast as though I was having a panic attack.

A Meeting with Destiny

Well I had been here for about a month or two, and for some reason I had a desire to write and see how Rosie was doing. You remember her; she was the older lady who was Blount's aunt that had waved at me from across the visiting room when I was at Pollock after my grandmother had passed. So I wrote her and asked if it was OK if I called her from time to time and maybe we could encourage each other. She wrote me back about two weeks later and responded by saying that she had prayed about it, and that she was led to believe it was OK for me to call her.

Once we started talking, amazingly I found myself calling her at least three times a week until she began taking up over 80 percent of my phone time every month! This woman had an anointing on her, and a love for others that was so profound and captivating until those fifteen-minute calls seemed like only fifteen seconds. She believed that God could and would do anything for His people if they were obedient and believed that He would.

She had financial as well as health issues, but none of those things moved her. She was one that believed God to be a healer as well as a provider. Every time I attempted to discuss or encourage

I'm Ready to Go

her concerning her inabilities or lack thereof, she always managed to somehow put the focus back on mine. And before I knew it, she had already begun praying for me, that God would supply my needs and fulfill my every desire.

The thing about writing a true story is that it compels you to tell all. That being said, I'm almost embarrassed to say that whenever this woman prayed for me under the anointing of the Holy Spirit, it would always bring about an unexpected attraction towards her. Could it be that our spirits became united in the midst of her praying for me? Or maybe it was because of the fact that I had been incarcerated for over nine years at that time, and the absence of a woman extending love towards me left me a little sensitive, to say the least.

As time passed, we became the very best of friends, sharing our every thought and concern, although I'm not ignorant to the fact that emotions had gotten involved—mine are mixed; hers aren't. She's hopeful that this road we're on will someday lead us to the altar. As for me, that's not a certainty, but her forever being a part of my life is. I've learned long ago how not to allow emotions to dictate life-changing choices that may have a permanent effect.

My first marriage took place in prison, and I thought I was doing it for all the right reasons. But the truth of the matter is it was built on deception as well as emotions, although this situation is a bit different because I'm fully persuaded that Rosie is everything that she portrays to be.

My biggest problem is this thing called preference, and unfortunately, I happen to have one. I've never really had a thing for women that much older than I am, among other things. But when I'm on the phone with her, nothing else seems to matter. It's when I'm all alone and I begin to think about the future, that's when I'm reminded about my past. The things that I used to appreciate the most in a woman, you know, the superficial things such as long hair, a curved body, etc., none of which could satisfy the very thing that my spirit man longed for.

Rosie satisfies that longing in my inner man in such a way that I'm lost for words when I begin to explain the essence of her spirit and character. To me she has become the standard for every woman whose endeavor is to excel in the Kingdom of God, and to be the servant, mother, and wife that the Lord has called them to be.

So why is it that I desire more concerning the natural, being persuaded that I'll receive less concerning the spiritual? I know that I have liberty in Christ when it comes to finding my wife, as long as she's in the Lord. But this is not easy for me, but I'm hoping it will become clearer once I've been delivered from prison and I'm out there with her.

When a man finds someone special he tends to want to introduce or share her with his family. The thing about that is, she's like a magnet. The anointing on her and the love she has for others just draw people to her. Amazingly, after a few conversations over the telephone with my mother, sister, and one of my aunts, they immediately fell in love with her and became advocates for her in pursuing her a husband, namely me. They presented me with every reason under the sun as to why age shouldn't be a factor, saying things like, "Age ain't nothing but a number"; "You should've had enough of those young women that meant you no good from the past"; or one of my personal favorites, "You know, your cousin married a man about twenty years older than she was."

Though they tried, I had a defense for their every offense. Although there may have been some validity to their claims, I refuse to let another choose my wife for me.

Denominations Clash

Well, things were heating up on the compound in the Christian community. As in every institution, there came a division in the body. A portion of the body believed in speaking in tongues, healing, and casting demons out of Christians. Others either didn't believe that those gifts were for today, or that they shouldn't be the central focus of a ministry to avoid possible stumbling blocks in the lives of other believers. Me personally, this was new territory, or doctrine, that I had not experienced for myself. Therefore I was more so inquisitive and open-minded.

Eventually I was approached by one of the brothers from the Pentecostal denomination who asked me if I had been baptized in the Holy Ghost with the evidence of speaking in tongues. I hesitated with my response, knowing that any response other than a definite "yes" would come with a full briefing on how to receive the baptism of the Holy Spirit.

But in that split moment I reasoned with myself and thought that even though the end result of going through this process could possibly raise questions with the brothers that I fellowship with on a daily basis that aren't of the Pentecostal persuasion, that if it was available, I wanted to experience everything that God has for me.

So after denying having this experience, Brother John began educating me on the importance of having this gift and how to receive it. He then handed me a piece of paper with a list of biblical Scriptures to study that would increase my faith and prepare me for this miracle. This brother believed that he had the calling of a prophet on his life, and that he perceived that I was called to be a teacher.

Now I had no confirmation concerning this brother's calling, but I did like the sound of him prophesying that I would be a teacher. Therefore I wanted him to be a true prophet. One thing that I was certain of: If God was to deliver me from this spirit of fear and use me to teach or preach with power before His people, as far as I'm concerned, that might just confirm that brother's calling to be a prophet.

Brother John also had another brother on the compound named Doc. We called him Apostle because he believed he was ordained by the Lord as one. This brother knew the Word so well and taught under the anointing of the Holy Spirit in such a way that one couldn't help but believe that he would someday pastor his own church, although he was a bit controversial being that he led the Pentecostal movement on the compound. I didn't always agree with all of his methods and how he dealt with the body as a whole, but one thing was certain: no one could deny the calling and anointing that was on his life.

As time passed, these brothers held healing, deliverance, and impartation services. They would invite brothers out with health problems, possible demon possession, and those that desired a prophetic word spoken over their lives regarding God's calling and divine purpose for their life. Besides reading it in God's Word and seeing it on television, I had never witnessed nor taken part in this type of demonstration of the power of God.

As the process began, I witnessed men falling to the floor after having hands laid on them and being prayed over, Brother Doc demanding that demons would come out of them by the power and authority of Jesus Christ. Many got up proclaiming that they had been delivered from the thing that had them bound. It was just as I remembered it to be when I had seen it on television in times past.

Although I was a sinner at that time, therefore I did have doubts as to whether it was all just a show. But now that I'm saved, I've come to believe that God can do everything that His Word says He can.

So the time had come for the brother to lay hands on me and for us to believe that the Lord would deliver me from the spirit of fear that plaques me whenever I attempt to speak before people, as well as deliverance from high blood pressure.

As he began to command these spirits to leave my body, I felt my body being driven to the floor with his hands. Although that left me a little perplexed, I continued to believe God for my healing and deliverance. But I did address my concerns to the brother days after the service, hoping that he would understand that I'd rather if he didn't push me down the next time. He said he didn't remember pushing me down, and that he would be more careful in the future.

Being Called into the Ministry

I have to commend the elders in the body as a whole. They were all very aggressive in helping brothers who they believed were called into the ministry by allowing them the opportunity of speaking in one way or another before the church for the purpose of preparing them for their calling and getting them comfortable with speaking in front of God's people.

Being that I had believed that God had called me into the ministry according to the Word that was spoken by the man of God and was confirmed by others, I made a vow to the Lord that whenever I'm called to speak before His people, I won't allow the spirit of fear to hinder me from going forward.

Satan was obviously listening in on our conversation, because one of the elders asked me to do the Scripture reading Sunday morning. As I sat in my chair anticipating being called up front, I began to experience another one of those panic attacks, only this time it was accompanied with excruciating pain from my chest around to my upper back. I immediately understood that I was in a spiritual warfare, and that Satan was trying to use what he knew to be a weakness and a hindrance of mine to keep me from entering into my destiny.

Trying hard not to be noticed, I began rebuking the enemy and speaking in my heavenly language that I believed the Lord had given me as I received by faith the baptism of the Holy Spirit. In the midst of that, I slowly began to stretch from side to side. Realizing that the pain had begun to subside, I gave God glory for giving me the victory over my first known encounter with the enemy.

As I was called up to read a Scripture, God gave me a word from it to encourage His people with. Even though it wasn't easy, it worked out beautifully. I realized that I didn't do it in my own strength, and that I must always rely on the power of God in order to accomplish the work of God.

As I continued to prepare myself for the work of the Lord, God used the eldership mightily in providing a platform for His upcoming ministers to exercise their gifts and callings. They were given the liberty to start having exhortations on every second and third Monday of the month. They would allow three brothers that were believed to be called into the ministry, after preparing beforehand, to give a fifteen- to twenty-minute exhortation each. It was on the night of my second exhortation that I found Brother John's prophecy concerning my calling to be confirmed.

God took over that night and demonstrated His power through me in such a way that left me in a state of awe for days. Everyone in the chapel gave God glory for what He had done on that night. Never again did I doubt the fact that God had called me into the ministry.

Although Satan continued to use the spirit of fear to keep me from wanting to speak before God's people, I came to realize that even in the face of fear, God's Word, work, and will would prevail. God had even seen fit to move a brother and long-time preacher of His Word that I met in Edgefield years ago in the cell with me. I knew that it was just part of the process that God was using to get me ready to go home.

You talk about a brother that knows the Word of God and never gets tired of talking! But I was thankful for him, and saw him as a great asset towards my endeavor to leave prison prepared for the work of the Lord.

6
A Friend Who Became My Enemy Is My Friend

In the process of time, my mind would tend to drift at times on an old friend that the government scared and pressured into testifying against me. She was this young lady named Priscilla. I wanted her to know that I understood why she did what she did and that I held no ill will against her. So I began trying to contact her in an effort to release her from any possible guilt that she may have had concerning my trial.

But what's crazy about remembering her is that there's some bad memories that are attached to even the thought of her that I've unsuccessfully tried to cleanse from my conscience. Since I'm thinking about how foolish I was and how could I have been so deep in sin, I may as well convey these embarrassing thoughts to you.

I was about twenty-five years old and in a marriage that never should have taken place. I was also involved in extramarital affairs, as was my wife. But there was this one young lady in particular that I was involved with named Priscilla that I really cared for. So there came a day when I was about to do something that I had not planned on doing; something very stupid and would not be forgotten.

My wife came to me one day and said that she wanted to go to the casino with my aunt and asked me for a hundred dollars. So I gave it to her and they were on their way. About thirty minutes later I received a call from Priscilla asking me to come and pick her up. She was one that I enjoyed being with, so it wasn't long before we were in the car together.

It was maybe about 8:30 at night when I remembered that I had left something at home that I needed to go back and pick up. As we pulled up in the driveway, I asked her if she wanted to come in for a few minutes, knowing that my reason for inviting her in was to show off my nice home. So I began to take her on a tour of the house and I could tell that she was impressed.

Finally we made it to the master bedroom, where my wife and I slept. That was about the second or third worst mistake of my life. For a moment, it seemed like the danger of being in that room, or the house for that matter, became an instant turn-on for two fools void of the voice of reason. Before I knew it, we were in bed as though we didn't have a care in the world. My pager was going off left and right, but I was too caught up to even look and see who it could be.

About ten minutes later the room door opened and the lights came on, and all I could do was call my wife's name. In a split second I thought to myself, this has got to be a nightmare and I had better wake up really fast because I know that my wife keeps the Glock 9mm that I bought her in her purse at all times. So whether I was dreaming or foolish enough to have allowed something like this to happen in real life, I knew that I had better jump up quick and grab her. One thing was certain—I didn't want to die in a dream or reality.

So with what appeared to be superhero-type speed, I had jumped up and grabbed her and wrestled her to the floor while Priscilla managed to put on most of her clothes and storm past my aunt, who was sitting in the living room. All I could think about at that time was that I should have given her more than just a hundred dollars. Maybe she wouldn't have lost so quickly at the casino!

Boy, was I stupid. I could have even checked my pager and realized that it was her calling me to tell me that they were on their way home. Even if I would have gotten out of the house before she made it home, what was I to do about the bed linen and the scent of another woman all over the room? I tell you the truth; sin will take you farther than you're willing to go, and keep you there longer than you're willing to stay. Once that nightmare was over, we decided to stay together for all the wrong reasons.

You would think that I had seen the last of Priscilla. How about the two of us eventually got back together, and only a couple of years later my wife asked me for money so she could go to the casino with my cousin? Well, that was the same day Priscilla and I were going to visit some of her relatives, only we had to go the same way that my wife would go to get to the casino. Well, I thought that I would be smart and give her about an hour head start. Besides that, I figured

A Friend Who Became My Enemy Is My Friend

I'd drive one of the cars off my car lot that she wasn't familiar with.

Well, as we were headed out around the time I thought she should already be there, as we were coming off of the off ramp, we literally pulled about two cars ahead of my wife's car. Although I didn't recognize her at first, somehow Priscilla did. All she could say was, "Oh, my God. That's your wife behind us!" Here I am reliving part two of a once-forgotten nightmare.

While looking through my side mirror, I noticed her car gaining speed as though it, or she, for that matter, was suspicious of something and just had to figure it out. As I remembered having an odd-shaped head, I thought that maybe she had spotted it already, not to mention the dealer tag on the back of the car revealing that it belonged to a car lot. The only thing I could think of at that moment was to ease the palm of my hand around the back of my head, hoping to cover up the flatness of it.

By that time, I was in the far right lane and she was in the next lane to my left, less than a car length from me. At this point, all I could think about was that Glock 9mm that she keeps with her. Realizing that I couldn't outrun her in the car I was driving, as she came within about two feet from being side by side with me, undoubtedly trying desperately to confirm whether or not it was really me, I did what the average man in my position would do—started praying.

At that very moment, out of nowhere came this rest stop. I don't ever remember it being there, unless I was too spaced out at the moment to remember. Anyway, I calmly veered to the right into the rest area, while my left hand remained on the back of my head with a slight adjustment to cover the side of my face. Looking in my side mirror, I saw my wife in a dilemma, being unable to get over in the right lane because of ongoing traffic and unable to stop due to traffic behind her moving at a rapid speed. She made the decision to floor it in an attempt to get off at the next exit, hoping to get back to the off ramp that would lead her back to the rest stop where I was. It was like we were playing a game of chess and it was my next move.

So I floored it as well, spotting a break in the highway on the far left side that would take me back towards home. Driving as fast as I could, anxious to get back to safety, my cell phone rang; it was my wife. After it stopped ringing, my pager started vibrating. Once I reached my destination, dropped Priscilla off, and parked the car in an apartment complex with plans to sell it first thing in the morning, I called my wife. And with much debate, I stuck to those infamous words of old: "Baby, it wasn't me."

Being in a confused state, she changed her mind about going to the casino and decided to go home. So I agreed to meeting her there. That night was never brought up again, and she never knew that it was me—at least until now. So my friend, I'm sorry for that night and whatever part that I played in our having an unsuccessful marriage.

Now that you know the type of relationship Priscilla and I had in the past, I can go forward by saying that I was able to get a message to her on how I felt towards what was said by her at my trial. She responded by sending me her address. I guess she wanted to hear it from me personally. Although that wasn't expected, I praised the Lord for the opportunity to share with her God's grace and love for her.

Once she had received my letter, she wrote me back thanking me for forgiving her, and giving me a brief description of the burden that had been lifted from her that she had to carry for so many years.

Although I'm sure it had gotten easier for her as time went by, still I know the games that the government tends to play on a person's mind, she being twenty-one years old at the time with one child, no job, no finances nor family support, with the knowledge of how the government operates or the strength to stand in their presence. Not to mention the fact that she could go to prison for a very long time for trying to protect and defend a married man who in her mind will never leave his wife for her.

Many people in my situation probably wouldn't forgive her out of selfishness and bitterness, not realizing that if they were put in her position most likely would've made the same choices. The process is simple; the government tells you that you'll receive twenty years in which you'll do eighteen straight without parole, or you tell the truth and go home. Ninety-eight percent of the people choose to go home, which is one reason why the government has about a 99 percent conviction rate. Overall, a small percent are mentally tough enough to defy the odds and hope for a better chance on appeal. After realizing that there wasn't much of a chance after losing their appeals, a portion of that percentage regrets their decision to go to trial.

So no, I don't fault her. Instead I fault a biased system that would have the audacity to give an individual up to a life sentence without the possibility of parole for a nonviolent crime. That almost seems demonic to me—to live in a country that claims to believe in the only true and righteous God, a God of mercy and love, yet we don't possess any of His characteristics. I can literally write for days concerning this broken system, but that's for another book.

So Priscilla sent me her phone number and asked me to call her because she didn't like to write, which is just a polite way of saying that she's lazy. Well, only weeks later, my friend had lost her mother, and I've got to tell you, Priscilla had the sweetest mother that a person could ask for. Besides that, they were the very best of friends. So therefore one can only imagine the pain that she had to endure. Who knows? Maybe my timely entrance back into her life was for a bigger calling than either one of us knew. More than anything, she could use a friend and the comforting Word of God.

While elaborating about my old friend and our newfound relationship, I would be remiss if I didn't take this opportunity to acknowledge that I turned forty-two years old on today, April 7, 2010, and I just feel great about that; to God be the glory!

Well lately I've been finding myself looking forward to calling Priscilla. Ministering to her seems to bring me unspeakable joy. I can't help but to think about how this could end; I mean the fact that she could some day become saved and possibly a mighty woman of God. That thought alone made me more zealous to want to talk with her as often as I could.

The downside to that meant I would have to call my friend Rosie less. Knowing that would disappoint her, I considered the possibility of just how great the reward would be if Priscilla had found the Lord during our time of getting to know one another again. What an awesome testimony that would be!

Speaking of getting to know her again, I was really impressed with the way she's matured over the years. Even her son turned out to be a really good kid, doing well in school and very athletic. Priscilla is a manager at a restaurant, and it's been over eleven-and-a-half years and she hasn't had another child and doesn't want another one either.

I'm truly fascinated with the reality of how time, accompanied with difficulty, tends to change a person to a certain extent. I remember when Priscilla was one of the prettiest young women in town. And because of her rare beauty, she saw no need to get a job. She felt that it was a man's duty to take care of her. Some would say she was a gold digger, but I beg to differ. Even though she refused to work, and wasn't shy when it came down to asking for what she wanted, she didn't want much. She was just a pretty little around-the-way girl that lived a simple life.

But that little boy of hers; he was only about four years old, but he had a mouth like Richard Pryor. He would cuss so bad until I became like a spy, seeking for the chance or opportunity for Priscilla to leave me alone with him. I had literally begun to envision the pleasure it would bring me just to pinch him until he started to cry.

I had it all planned out. Once I was satisfied and felt that he had suffered enough, I was going to try and bribe him with some candy and maybe a few dollars not to tell his mother. Now I know that I was wrong to even be thinking along those lines, but I just felt somehow he had to be stopped. So now when I see the transformation that has taken place in both of their lives, it makes me laugh.

Anyway, we've been talking a lot about the Lord, and she seems to be OK with that. She tells me that she can see herself living for the Lord some day, but like most of us, she's just not ready yet. But I vowed that I wouldn't give up on her, at least until the Lord tells me that my season of planting was up and that it was time to allow someone else to water. Until then, I continued steadfast in prayer on her behalf, that the Lord wouldn't allow her to see death and continue to draw her until she answers His call.

I was sharing the Gospel with her so much until the Holy Spirit had to rebuke me and let me know that I was choking her with the Word, and that I needed to put a balance on the content of our conversations. So one night I was reminded of our past faults, particularly concerning that night when a thing called sin had led the two of us into me and my wife's bedroom. Before I could get the words all the way out, she immediately stopped me with an attitude of disgust and shame, forbidding me to go on any further. She asked me if I would change the subject. Continuously being impressed with how she's matured over the years, I graciously agreed.

As I reflect back on that night, Priscilla was not only unashamed of what we had done, but she was hopeful that this would surely end my marriage and pave the way for us to be together as husband and wife. So for that subject to be too sensitive for us to even talk about let's me know that she's definitely not the same Priscilla that I once knew, although her hopes of us being together in that way some day wasn't out of the question.

She was someone whom I cared a lot for, even though I intentionally withheld that knowledge from everyone around me for the purpose of appearing to have everything under control. So I'm thankful that I'm no longer bound to having to live a lie.

Anyway, her mother, who had recently passed, came up a lot in our conversations, due to her having to deal with the frequent pain of missing her. I lost my grandmother years ago, so I knew what she was going through, only I had the Lord to help me through the pain. So it hurt me to see her go through her loss without the comforting presence of God.

But I did all that I could in order to help ease the pain. I prayed with her and shared Scriptures with her that confirmed God's love for her and His desire to want to reveal His plans and purpose for her life. I sent her a couple of books with words of encouragement for her to read in times of despair. I even had a portrait done of her—anything to create a smile that would last. But I knew that I had my work cut out for me. It's not easy losing a mother—especially one who was as sweet as hers. But I'll keep trying; that's what love does.

7
Looking for a Sign

Well, as God has been preparing me for the ministry, I've been sensing in my spirit that it was my season, and that the Lord was about to reveal His hand of deliverance in the midst of my situation. In times past, I've attempted to contact quite a few Civil Rights organizations, searching for someone, anyone, who would take interest in my case, and take the evidence that God had given me and put it in the hands of someone with the authority and the integrity to respond to the findings in an unbiased and just way.

I sought help from organizations such as the American Civil Liberties Union (ACLU), The Innocence Project, TOPS, The National Action Network, etc., all to no avail. I had come to realize that all of these prominent organizations would no doubt try and steal the spotlight and the glory from the God who made it all possible. So it was obvious that the Lord had allowed them all to turn a deaf ear to my cause.

Now that I had forsaken all for the will of the Lord and had begun to aggressively prepare myself to be used by Him in a mighty way for His glory once I'm released, I began to expect and to look for the manifestation of God's delivering power in my situation. I also believed that it wasn't a coincidence that we now have our first black president and attorney general of the United States, but that it was by divine appointment.

Not long after they had been in office, I observed a young man having a beautiful portrait done of President Barak Obama. He was hoping that this gift, along with a brief summary of his case, particularly the injustice that he believed the government displayed in his case, would reach the president and result in a favorable response on his behalf. After sending his package out by certified mail and receiving a return receipt, he had hoped for the best. After months of no response, not even a thank you from a staff member, it seemed that all hope was lost. Although it appeared to be a good idea at the time, one may think that it was done with the purpose of using the portrait as a persuasion tool or possibly seen as flirting with bribery. Therefore I couldn't see myself taking that route.

Ironically, after only about two weeks later, out of nowhere I was given the inspiration to have a portrait done of Attorney General Eric Holder, expressing my gratitude and congratulating him on becoming the first black attorney general of the United States, along with a brief summary of my case and expressing the injustice that I had suffered. I was very hesitant of having this done, not knowing whether or not it was of God. It had only been a couple of weeks when my heart was set against it. What had changed since then? Or had I forgotten that the brother before me was unsuccessful with getting a response?

While pondering on the matter, I decided to call one of my aunts to see how she was doing. Surprisingly she began to express her admiration for President Obama and Attorney General Eric Holder for their accomplishments. She's been a civil rights activist all of her life, so I could only imagine what this meant to her.

As she continued to elaborate and express her excitement over these two men making history, she said something that left me speechless, yet brought confirmation to the very thing that I had been seeking God for concerning Attorney General Eric Holder. She told me that he was married to one of my cousins on my grandfather's side of the family. Although I didn't know this cousin personally, I realized that God couldn't have given me a more profound sign that the inspiration of having the portrait done and sending it to him, accompanied with the evidence that the Lord had given me, was definitely from Him.

While waiting on the completion of the portrait, the Lord began to reveal to me that there was a specific way that I was to prepare and send the package. Once the portrait was complete, I was to take the evidence that the Lord had given me, along with a personal letter addressed to Attorney General Eric Holder, and put it all in one box. Then I was to send it certified to my ninety-three-year-old grandfather, and have him send it certified to Attorney General Eric Holder.

After my grandfather had sent the package and received the return receipt about ten days later, I was to then wait patiently for a favorable response.

As I was waiting, the enemy did all he could to make me doubt that these were instructions from the Lord and that it was my season for a breakthrough, using all of the attempts that I made in the past; seeking various organizations for help but to no avail; including thoughts of the brother before me who attempted the exact same thing, but failed. While in this spiritual battle, I continued to cast down every thought or imagination that tried to exalt itself against the knowledge of God.

Not many days later, I received a letter in the mail from the Department of Justice. It was from the director under Attorney General Eric Holder. He acknowledged that my package was received and stated the nature of my claims, and that it was pending a response. Now I don't know about you, but I was overwhelmed with joy, being fully persuaded that this was the Lord's doing and that the victory was already won.

Show Me the Money

Well, it's been about six months now, and I've been waiting patiently in the Lord for the response of a lifetime, also having been counseled by the Holy Spirit to only share this with a faithful few. Sometimes it's not wise to reveal a matter until after it has come to pass. Not everyone is happy with hearing your good fortune unless they can help you spend it. And Satan is looking for someone who is willing to be used to thwart the plans of God, although I did share the news with certain members in my family. I know that they so desperately want to believe that it's almost over. Being that I've been telling them it's almost over since the very beginning when the Lord had first revealed to me that He would deliver me has probably left them with the Missouri mentality. So even though they seem excited about it, I still hear what they're not saying, which is I'm going to have to show them in order for them to believe it.

I also sense a similar mindset with some of them regarding the genuineness of my changed life and whether or not it will last once

I return home. I know that they want to believe the sincerity of my salvation, but past history has taught them differently.

We men come to prison so often and profess to be saved only to get back out and back into the same lifestyle that led us to prison the first time. Our ignorance and weakness have nullified the saving power of God in the minds of our families and loved ones on the outside.

Some of us seem to think we can fake salvation while in prison in an effort to fool God into delivering us out of prison, being blinded to the fact that God knows the thoughts and intents of every man's heart. Although some are sincere about their salvation when they get out, they just aren't rooted and grounded or prepared for the temptations and trials that will come to test and try their faith.

I once fell into this category, coming out of prison for the first time, having been saved for a little over a year. Before coming home, I married a long-time girlfriend who was pregnant with my child. Knowing in my heart that she wasn't truly saved, I went against the will of God and married her anyway for selfish reasons. Even though I fought to hold on to God's unchanging hand, the enemy used her to draw me back into my old life that I once knew. Therefore, I can identify with family members and loved ones when they're not convinced that we've truly found the Lord.

But I've been with God for over eleven years now, and I've come to a place in life where I'm not trying to convince anyone of the authenticity of my salvation. I am who I am by the grace of God, and come hell or high water, I will not turn back. I have nowhere else to go. I'm like Peter, Lord; where else can I go? You have the words to eternal life. Therefore everyone who once knew the old me will come to know that God still saves, even in prison.

So I exhort every man in prison who professes to know the Lord to take heed to these sayings, and thoroughly examine themselves to see whether or not they're truly in the faith. Once this truth has been established, I believe that the next step would be to check the level of your spiritual maturity by the Word of God.

Some may say that I'm not that bad off, but we know that it's the little foxes that spoil the vine. We can't expect for God to deliver an unprepared mediocre Christian out of prison knowing that their fall will not only lead them back to prison, but will also give more credence to the jailhouse religion stigma that has been attached to the average brother that the Lord saves in prison.

A Get-Out-of-Jail-Free Card, Only It's Not Free

We have to realize that we have much to do with the Lord choosing to deliver us from prison early. We have the privilege of allowing ourselves to be delivered from prison early by the hand of God. Although we can't dictate when, we can shorten or even lengthen the process by our aggressive endeavor to grow in God or lack thereof.

The Bible tells us in II Chronicles chapter 16 verse 9 that "the eyes of the Lord roam to and fro throughout the whole earth, to shew Himself strong in the behalf of them whose heart is perfect toward Him." This simply means that the Lord is strategically looking in every place, every crack or crevice, seeking to find a heart that has been prepared for the Master's use; one that is walking in the *agape* love of God, battle tested and able to go through the adversities of life without wavering and praising God in the midst of it, so that when God sees you, He can say that My son or My daughter is ready to be delivered; ready to go out into the world and to show forth My character in such a way that others will look upon him and be able to identify him with Me; ready to proclaim My goodness and to tell all that will listen that his God is a deliverer and a lover of your soul.

Now let's establish this principle of early release from prison by turning backwards to chapter 7, verse 14 of the same book, where we find God instructing Solomon concerning His people. He says that "if my people, which are called by My name, shall humble themselves, and pray, and seek My face, and turn from their wicked ways; then will I hear from heaven, and will forgive their sin, and will heal their land." Now this word *heal* is synonymous with *deliverance*, just as *land* is with *problems* or *situations*.

As we keep that in mind, let's move ahead to chapter 33 verses 12 and 13. Before I expound on these two verses, allow me to give a brief summary of this chapter. Here we find that Manasseh succeeded his father, Hezekiah, as King of Jerusalem at the age of twelve years old. Unlike his father, Manasseh was evil and did worse than the heathen had done. He killed innocent people, caused his children to pass through the fire, dealt in all sorts of witchcraft, and he taught God's people to do the same.

But the Bible tells us that the Lord spoke to Manasseh concerning his ways but he refused to listen. So the Lord sent the police to arrest Manasseh and took him among the thorns, and bound him with fetters, and threw him in the Babylon prison. Ain't it just like God to send us a warning before destruction? And like Manasseh, it's just like us to ignore it, and to find ourselves in prison with no one to call on but the Lord.

Now in verses 12 and 13, the Bible tells us that when Manasseh was in affliction, "he besought the Lord his God, and humbled himself greatly before the God of his fathers, and prayed unto him, and he was intreated of him, and heard his supplication, and brought him again to Jerusalem into his kingdom. Then Manasseh knew that the Lord he was God." And he commanded all of Judah to serve the Lord God of Israel.

Even though Manasseh was a wicked king, it's clear that he knew the instructions of the Lord. If we were to consider the format of his confession, we would find that it parallels with the Lord's instructions to Solomon concerning His people back in chapter 7 verse 14. Manasseh had met the necessary requirements that resulted in an early release from prison that was established by God Himself. And the works that he did once he was released from prison demonstrate the authenticity of his conversion and spiritual maturity.

Because God doesn't reveal to us our new release date, we tend to get distracted by the television, the weight pile, sports, what's going on in the free world, etc., and we unknowingly prolong our stay in prison. The recipe is simple: Believe that the Lord God is a deliverer and that He desires to deliver you for His glory.

Get God's attention, not as though you have to, because He's an all-knowing God, but in the sense of seeking Him in prayer concerning His Word of deliverance, and coming into covenant with Him concerning it. Spend much time in His presence as well as around mature men of God. This will allow those little foxes in our lives that I spoke on earlier to be illuminated, and to give you a sense of urgency to deal with them.

As you continue to do this and stay in God's Word, you will not only come to know the full counsel of God, but what your calling and purpose are as well. As you allow God to prepare, equip, and groom you for your calling, He will begin creating opportunities for you to exercise it. And once you've been proven in your level of love and character, equipped yourself in the Word, and prepared to walk in your calling, I believe that ignites God concerning His Word to begin to put in motion His plan of deliverance for you.

8
Family Crisis

Well, as I was speaking on family and their warranted doubts concerning whether or not we've been truly saved, it caused me to consider my very own family and the state of mind that they're now in, and the task that's set before me. I come from a family where I'm pretty much loved by everyone, but not everyone in the family can honestly say that.

The Bible tells us that money is a root of all kinds of evil, and my family's actions over the years do attest to that. Some are breeding hatred one towards the other, taking each other back and forth to court over money that doesn't belong to either of them, while others haven't spoken in years—all because of money. The question in my mind is, how do I approach this crisis once I'm out, being that I'm close at heart to all of them?

My mission is simple. My earnest desire for them is to see them saved. Therefore I will lovingly proclaim the Gospel of Jesus Christ in their hearing, coupled with praying daily for their souls, as I live a life of holiness while walking in victory in every aspect of life. But I will not allow my love for them to cause me to deviate from the course that the Lord has set before me.

While considering the possibility that after the Lord has used me to sound the alarm and my loved ones may fail to wake up, or to bear fruits of repentance, I know that eternity in hell awaits them. So I'm looking unto God for another miracle, and that is to save my family.

I'm also blessed to have a son and three daughters who are dear to my heart. Although only one of my daughters professes to be saved, and even she needs to be brought into a level of spiritual maturity, still I'm hopeful concerning them becoming children of the Most High due to my accessibility to them and their hearts not being hardened.

There's another part of my family on my father's side that has lived only two blocks away in the same neighborhood that I've dared to even call family until now. My father neglected me from birth until I became an adult and decided to reach out to him. Even then there were only a few visits from me before I sort of grew past trying to establish a relationship with him. But there was no legitimate reason for me failing to establish a relationship with my brothers and sisters by him.

Many times they attempted to reach out to me in the sense of speaking or saying something like, "You look just like your brother." Although I do remember coming to one of my brothers' aid once in an effort to help his mother find him a good lawyer. But it hurts me today to admit the truth as to why I never took the time to get to know them.

I was ashamed to be identified with them, thinking I was better than they were because they were poor and people treated me as though I was somebody just because I lived a flamboyant lifestyle, when in all actuality, I was a nobody built up on false pride.

Now after being in prison for several years, I was cut to the heart when one of my brothers sent a thousand dollars to my account and hundreds of beach pictures that he took the time to take, just for me. After talking with him on the telephone, he asked me if I needed any more, as well as committing himself to raising forty thousand dollars in order to retain a lawyer for my appeal, although he was arrested and sent to prison before he was able to do it because he was trying to get it illegally. Besides that, the Lord wasn't going to permit my deliverance to come by those means. Still, at that moment I felt very small and unworthy of the love that my brother extended towards me. Never again will I exalt myself above measure and become self-deceived into thinking that I'm better than anyone.

A life of sin has no limits to where it will take you, and sometimes you never get back. I'm grateful to God that I was able to. So one of my first stops once I'm out is to see about him and the rest of my family on my father's side.

Tried Faith

Well, I was a little tired after getting off work, so I decided to sit on my bunk and read the Mobile papers that a young man from my neighborhood brings me. After only about five minutes, I ran across an article that really tested my faith. Now I know that the Lord has already given me the evidence that would free me from prison. But there's one piece of evidence in particular concerning one of the prosecutors on my case.

He had committed perjury against me, and for some unknown reason, it was said in open court that he was no longer employed by the government. I knew that if this statement was found to be true that it would only strengthen my case.

I was inclined to believe this statement to be true, well, at least until after I had read this news article which not only confirmed the fact that he was still employed by the government as a prosecutor, but he was recently promoted as head prosecutor by President Obama.

Now I've got to tell you that the enemy had a field day with this temporary reality by using it for the sole purpose of trying to cause me to entertain the spirit of doubt and fear. The very thought of this prosecutor being promoted by the president had caused me to consider whether or not politics would hinder or slow down the process of my deliverance. Being that the president exalted this man based on his record and reputation, I assume, what would be said concerning his judgment of character once my allegations are found to be true by the Justice Department? And would this potential dilemma persuade him into manipulating the situation that would produce an outcome that's less favorable towards me?

After the enemy had thrown everything including the kitchen sink at me, I began to encourage myself by being reminded of who it was that said He would deliver me. Who gave me this evidence? Who was it that said that the king's heart is in His hand? And finally, who am I and whose am I? A son of the Most High God.

Like the children of Israel, God gives us our promised land. However, through much fighting do we enter in and possess it; although we take comfort in the fact that every fight is fixed and we are the victors. Therefore I continue to wait in God until my departure from this wilderness and my arrival into my promised land.

Watch Them Foxes

Well it's a little quieter here in the Christian community since Brother Doc has gone home and his brother has taken over as the head elder over the Pentecostal denomination. Still there's division and a lack of unity in the Christian body as a whole. Any time you begin to exalt a particular denominational persuasion in the midst of a diverse body of believers, as opposed to walking in the spirit of love as mature believers, there will be division.

The Bible tells us to follow after the things which make for peace, and things wherewith one may edify another. We as believers are so adamant about promoting one doctrine above another, yet we struggle with operating in the level of power which gives us the victory over those little foxes in our lives.

When I use the term "little foxes," I'm referring to those little pet sins that we tend to hold on to while undermining their potential to stagnate, if not cripple you, from moving into the very plans and purposes that God has ordained for your life. You know, things such as constantly watching TV shows that promote sexual promiscuity or other things that you're already struggling with, such as concealing food and sneaking it out of the kitchen. Although they appear small on the surface, they have serious implications when it comes to damaging your testimony, causing a stumbling block for other young believers, or even possibly hindering an unbeliever from coming to the Lord.

While practicing these seemingly harmless little sins on a regular basis, our spirit begins to lose its sensitivity and eventually becomes callous. When we've reached that stage, this way of life becomes normal to us, to the point where we're no longer concerned with who's watching us pack food underneath our clothing, or the possibility of the CO pulling us over and shaking us down only to find the stolen goods. Instead of being embarrassed or our spirit being grieved, we're more concerned about the loss of the stolen goods.

Family Crisis

But yet we're promoting our Pentecostal persuasion, which includes being baptized in the Holy Ghost, speaking in tongues, casting out demons, operating in the calling and gifts of the Spirit, and walking in the power of God Almighty. Yet we can't muster up enough power that will give us the victory over the smallest sins.

When Paul was addressing the Corinthian church, he put them on notice that he was coming to them shortly, and would know their state—not their speech, but their power. He went on to say that the Kingdom of God is not in word, but in power. So therefore, those who profess to have matured beyond the stage of infancy or babes in Christ are without excuse, being that an inexhaustible reservoir of power has been made available to all who desire to be an overcomer.

When we begin to exalt denomination over character, we stand the chance of flirting with a religious spirit, and we become no different than the various religious sects that were in opposition to the mission of our Lord and Savior Jesus Christ—a mission that was driven by a profound love for the world—and that we all might have the opportunity to have fellowship with the Father and to be one with Him, just as He and His Son are one. So when we allow denomination to separate us, it demonstrates our failure to walk in love. As a result, that diminishes our known symbol to the world that identifies us with Christ, which is our love for one another.

Doc's brother continues to promote both of their convictions, whether right or wrong. Unfortunately, they've gained total control over the will of the younger brethren that they've reared up under Pentecostal persuasion. Not only are they forbidden to attend regular Sunday morning service with the Christian body as a whole, but they've also convinced them that they're in error if they sow any financial seeds or monthly tithes to any ministry or church on the outside. Instead they should sow all financial gifts directly to them, and for quite some time now that's exactly how it's been done.

They are literally making merchandise out of these younger brothers. And to come against this erroneous teaching creates a wedge between you and the very brothers that you're trying to protect, which I've come to experience firsthand. So the unspoken slogan here is if you have a problem with our leader, then you have a problem with us. I say this with great sorrow that this has gone beyond denominational persuasion, and even religion. I have now found myself engaged in a spiritual warfare against the spirit of a cult. Prayerfully I've realized that the most effective weapon against this spirit is to continue to walk in love in the midst of my brethren.

It wasn't long before one of the older brethren who was under the influence of this cult spirit approached me and said the Lord revealed to him that I genuinely have a love for him. Being that I sang in the choir, he asked when the next time I would be singing. I thought that was an odd question being that we both knew that I was a background singer and not a lead singer.

Immediately the Spirit revealed to me that he missed coming to church and wanted to come back, but he was afraid of what his Pentecostal brothers might say. So I understood that he was trying to get me to invite him to church so that he would have an excuse for being there. After all, although I was basically an outsider at the time, I still attended their services at the expense of trying to keep my communication with the brethren going.

So I asked, "Brother, why don't you come to church with me this Sunday?"

"Are you inviting me?" he asked.

"Of course!" I said.

He responded by saying, "Then I'll be there," along with a sigh of relief as though a burden had been lifted.

Sunday morning came, and we both had an awesome time singing praise and worship songs along with the choir. He also enjoyed the message that the Lord gave to the chaplain to bless the body with. He was overwhelmed by the confirmations he received from the sermon, which lined up with a word that he believed God had given him prior to coming to church.

Afterwards my Jamaican Christian brother had no regrets and looked forward to the next Sunday when he would be able to experience it once again.

It was the start of a beautiful day, at least until after lunch when he met with his Pentecostal brothers for their regular time of fellowship. It was obvious that there was some serious espionage going on inside the chapel on behalf of their sect, due to the fact that they were waiting to bring my brother up on charges for attending

Sunday services, which he was forbidden to attend. Not only did they recommend that he step away from their ministry, but they also suggested that the devil used me to invite him.

The Lord revealed to me that day to no longer lend my presence to their services, knowing that I didn't support their heresies. This was not their practice from the beginning. They loved going to Sunday services when they were in charge or leading the worship services until there was a change in chaplaincy and the services became more chaplain-led.

Their excuse for leaving the church and taking their followers with them was that the Holy Ghost was taken out of the church, as opposed to telling the truth, which was that they couldn't stand to humble themselves and sit down after repeatedly exalting their self-given titles of an apostle and prophet and proclaiming that it was God's order that the church be run by them, and that it was the chaplain's job to assist and support their God-given agenda. So to put their excuse for leaving in a nutshell was basically this little thing that God hates called pride.

Now my Jamaican brother is at liberty to attend every Christian service and he considers that to be of great gain. As for my Pentecostal brothers whom I love dearly, well they've lost the attendance of two sincere brothers, not to mention a significant amount of tithes and offerings from their Jamaican brother. But we both remain prayerful that the Lord will bring correction to our brothers that will lovingly bring them back into right fellowship with the Christian body as a whole. We all await their return, and look forward to embracing them.

A Father's Day Visit

Well, it's Sunday weekend before Father's Day, and I've just spent two days in the visiting room with my mother, two of my aunts, one named Ursela and the other Ellen, who is a long-time evangelist, and last but certainly not least, my ninety-four-year-old granddaddy, whom I resemble in appearance as well as certain characteristics. Man, I had such a wonderful time out there with them.

My Aunt Ellen just happens to be a Christian comedian who never stops talking while we never stopped laughing. The first thing she did when she walked in the door was run towards me undoubtedly to hug me. As I opened my arms to embrace her, surprisingly I found myself in a headlock receiving multiple blows to the head followed by a knee to the stomach.

Before I could catch my breath and ask the most sensible question I could think of, "What did I do?" she began shouting, "Why haven't you called me?" while constantly reaffirming that this fifty-six-year-old woman still can go.

After pleading with her and saying I was sorry, she finally gave in and turned me loose. I was just thankful the COs didn't threaten to ask her to leave or end my visit. But I laughed it off and vowed never to delay calling her again. I could almost imagine how far she'd go to get a laugh from her audience.

I'm thankful she has such a graceful talent, especially being that the court has granted her the responsibility of watching over my grandfather, who now lives with her after surviving about eleven silent strokes, which has caused him to lose his speaking ability and his ability to eat solid foods, among other ailments.

No doubt this illness is due to continuous stress from having to endure countless family feuds, which often involved his daughters, one against the other. Money was the center of 99.9 percent of the quarrels, and usually it was his money they were fighting over. And it has never been more heated up than it is at this present time. Therefore I praise God for my aunt's talent to make people laugh, particularly my grandfather. Lord knows I want to see him alive and well when I walk out of these prison doors.

Even though we had to play charades in order to figure out what he was trying to say, some things about my grandfather may never change, such as his unwavering desire to have sexual intercourse with a younger woman. He has always been a rather mannish old man, and even though he can't talk, he jokingly made it known through sign language that nothing has changed in that area.

I don't believe there is anything more strange than witnessing a ninety-four-year-old man making implications that he wants to lay with a woman, especially him being my grandfather, and a retired preacher. But he's my grandfather and I'm just so thankful that he's alive.

My mother doesn't say much. She reminds me of myself. She would rather listen than talk. But she made one thing very clear: it's time for me to come home, and I concur.

My Aunt Ursela, she's been having financial difficulties and marital problems for as long as I can remember, and I'm inclined to believe that it's more so linked to her failure to totally surrender to the Lord than anything. I get the impression that there's not much she won't do to obtain wealth, short of risking her life and freedom, of course. But we're very close, and I'm persuaded that I'll be able to help give her a different perspective on life once I'm out there with her.

My Aunt Ellen, although she's an evangelist and has been in the Lord for over twenty-five years now, I believe there are some things that need to be dealt with in her life that God may be glorified in a more excellent and profound way. If for nothing else, that our family may have a more identifiable pattern to follow; one that will help lead them to the Lord.

As we ended our visit, my aunt asked me to close us out in prayer. Once I was finished, nothing excited my grandfather more than to know that I was a praying man who reminded him of himself when he was once the prayer leader and a prayer warrior of Magnolia Baptist Church where I attended as a young boy until I became an adult.

It blessed me when they were leaving and I told them I would be home soon and he mumbled something that was interpreted by my aunt to mean that he knew it to be true because God had already revealed it to him. It brings me much comfort to know that my family is not worrying about me.

Children Never Outgrow Their Fathers

I understand that I'm not the only one doing this time. I know this affects everyone who loves me. Just the other day, I couldn't stop my twenty-two-year-old daughter from crying over the phone. It came out of nowhere. All I did was give her some advice concerning a personal issue, which I often do. And even though she's an adult now, she understands the need of having here father in her life.

I know I can't make up for lost time, but I feel the need to spend some quality time with my children, even before finding my wife once I'm out, being that I left them when they were between the ages of eight and twelve years old.

I received a recent e-mail from my youngest daughter, who will be twenty this year. The e-mail contained only three words: I need you. She was dealing with a personal issue concerning her mother's husband. He had run into some trouble with the law, and it seemed like he might be coming to prison if the Lord didn't intervene.

It's my prayer that God will, accompanied with him, surrendering his life to the Lord. Even though my daughter is not close to him, she's seen enough of federal agents walking in and out of her home throughout the years, taking loved ones with them, not knowing if they'll ever return. But I'm thankful to God that He has allowed us to build a father and daughter relationship that one can only dream of having under these circumstances. To God be the glory!

I discern a sense of trust and even refuge in their spirit when given the opportunity to counsel them during their time of despair. It's become abundantly clear to me that even though mothers are so important and desperately needed in a child's life, they could never be fathers. And this time apart from them has taught me that we are equally needed. Therefore, even in prison, we as fathers should create an atmosphere for our children that will produce a type of safe haven they can run to for shelter in a time of storm.

In order for us to do this, we have to first experience this kind of atmosphere with our very own Father, the Lord God Almighty. It's only through His love and wisdom that we're able to do this. Once we've exposed our children to this divine source of fatherly attributes which we had initially lost in the Garden through Adam, it will become natural for us to become their first person of contact in response to adversity.

Is There a Balm in Jesup?

Well, here I was on my way to work, just excited about life and looking forward to the future, when I ran into my best friend and brother in the Lord named Harold. He's this white guy in my unit that I've been fellowshipping with since the day I stepped on the compound. I can't talk to him without laughing. He's the funniest guy you'll ever meet, and he loves the Lord. Besides that, he's the reason for me writing this book.

One day he approached me with a perplexed look on his face. Then out of nowhere, he said, "Man, you're gonna think I'm crazy, but the Lord told me to tell you to write a book about the things that have happened in your case." He said he was reluctant to tell me this for fear of not wanting to sound crazy, but the Lord wouldn't leave him alone. So the rest was history.

Anyway, on this particular day, he had another strange look on his face, only this time he didn't look perplexed. It was more like he had seen a ghost. So he walked up to me, and without a moment's notice, he blurted out the words that a person is never prepared to hear coming from someone they're close to. He said, "Brother, I just left medical and the doctor said I've got cancer." He went on to say that he would be leaving soon to have surgery, then to a medical facility.

I was speechless for at least sixty seconds. He had been going through some excruciating pain for nearly a year now. But after having countless visits to the doctor, he was told that X-rays showed that he was only constipated. I've always found it difficult to get proper medical attention in prison. They seem to think that ibuprofen and laxatives are the answer to all of your problems. It's obvious that saving money is much more important than saving the lives of inmates. But I began to encourage him by reminding him of our Great Physician and Healer whom we serve, although I know it can be difficult holding on to faith while facing possible fatality.

To my surprise, that evening he was as joyful as he had ever been. He took the approach that whatever God allows is for his good and for God's glory. Whether healing or death, victory is his, and he demonstrated with power that the joy of the Lord was his strength.

Ever since then he's been back to his old self, funnier than ever. You can't tell me that my God isn't awesome! I believe that my brother's response to his crisis was a recipe for a miracle, and I'm looking forward to his praise report proclaiming that he shall live and not die.

A Birthday Prayer for My Ex

Well it's June 27, my ex-wife's birthday. It's three days before my son's birthday. Although I'm running late, I've decided to send her a card as I always do on her birthday. I know that she's going through some tough times right now, being that her husband is in jail facing federal charges. I've yet to cease from praying for them since hearing the news. I pray that the Lord will not only deliver him from his troubles, but also save the both of them in the process.

I've been away for nearly twelve years now, and her husband has always been there for my children when they had a need. For that I am grateful; and although I disagree with his method for getting wealth, he's earned my respect for doing that which I was unable to do for my children.

I remember about a year and a half ago when they were victims of a home invasion. I was angry with my wife for quite some time for not learning from the past, and choosing the same lifestyle that led many members of the family to federal prison—a choice that has also endangered their lives as well as the lives of my two children by a home invasion that could have been fatal.

I admit I was wrong for harboring resentment in my heart towards her. And for what it was worth, I did eventually apologize. I'm persuaded that my ex-wife is someone who has never believed my profession of faith in the Lord to be genuine. There was even a time in her anger towards me that she expressed her disbelief.

Although her assumptions are false, I understand her convictions. After all, she has witnessed my life as a sinner since she was fourteen years of age. Not to mention my short-lived life as a young Christian when we had first gotten married where I allowed the pressure of being unable to make her happy with a regular nine-to-five suffocate my zeal to please the Lord. Therefore her doubts are justified by the memories of the past.

But I know that she's heartbroken right now, having to relive the past of seeing a second husband face federal prison time. The Bible tells us to rejoice with them that rejoice, and weep with them that weep. I take no pleasure in her calamity. And even though I have a desire to write and encourage her, there's doubt that she may not take my sincerity to heart, instead thinking that I'm inwardly mocking her. As a result she'll feel worse than before.

Therefore I feel compelled not to alert her of my knowledge concerning her current adversities. So I continue to pray for her without ceasing, that the Lord will comfort her and be merciful unto her as well as her husband.

I've considered the content of my conversation or thoughts towards my ex-wife throughout this endeavor to tell my story, realizing that I may have painted a not-so-pretty picture of the nature and character of who she is. But let me go on record by saying that out of all the mistakes she's made, none could hold a candle to the ones I've made—not that I inspired to bring out the worst in her or she in me. It was just that greed for attractive things was found in the both of us, even at an early age, which kept us in bondage to them.

But I'm a witness that God is a deliverer of anything that a person is in bondage to. And just as He freed me from the power of it, He can do the same for her.

9
Satan's Attempt to Steal God's Glory

Well, I heard from my aunt today, the evangelist. She informed me that an old friend contacted her and left his phone number for me to call him. He was my cell mate when I was at Pollock USP. His name is Jay, and he thought he was God's gift to women. He claimed to have been a pimp on the street. You know, one who exploits women for money.

I called him to see how he was doing, and as expected, he seemed to be doing OK financially. He was reunited with his old girlfriend, who bought him a truck, as well as used her connections to land him a job driving 18-wheelers.

He's been out for over a year and a half now, but he's yet to get used to the outside world. He says the people are different now than they were before he went to prison.

Anyway, after we had gotten through all of the small talk, he had a proposition for me. He told me that his job driving trucks has afforded him the opportunity of meeting all types of people, particularly drug dealers. And he asked me if I was interested in having some of them set up by the Feds in exchange for a time cut.

Now the thing about this proposal is that if pursued and accomplished, it has no potential of bringing God glory. You can't just find someone to tell on in order to go home, and then say, "The Lord delivered me," when the truth of the matter is, God had nothing to do with it.

You can always tell when God's hand is in something; when man's hand isn't. Besides, God has brought me too far and has given me too much for me to forfeit His glory and give it to another.

Although his intentions seemed good, it was obvious he was unknowingly being used by the enemy in order to sabotage the very plans of God to bring me out of prison in such a way that one can't help but to concede that it was done by the power of God, for the purpose of bringing glory to His name and sinners to His Son.

So what the enemy meant for evil, the Lord turned it around and allowed me to use this opportunity to share with my friend what the Lord was about to do. And once He brings it to pass, I'm believing that the Lord will use this awesome testimony to bring him to want to know this mighty God I serve.

I tell you the truth, I'm just satisfied with Jesus alone. And I know that according to His Word, there's no good thing will He withhold from them that walk uprightly.

In Love with the Anointing

It has been well over a couple of months since I've last spoken with my friend Priscilla. I sometimes think about her, though, and wonder how she's doing. I made a choice to stop calling her because of her passion for things she wanted in life that just wouldn't come quickly enough, such as a husband, etc.

Unfortunately, these cares of life were drowning out the Word of God that I had been sharing with her and causing it to be unfruitful. But I believe that God's seed had been planted, as I occasionally send her some words of encouragement. And I am believing God to send others across her path to water the seed that has been sown into her heart, which would some day grace me with the opportunity of hearing her say, "I'm saved." Until then, my prayers are forever with her.

Of course, it's just the opposite with my friend and sister in the Lord, Rosie. I'm actually beginning to wonder, could this much older woman some day become my wife? All of these years that I've been divorced, I've always imagined my next wife being this beautiful young woman who loves the Lord. Now I'm finding myself being in love with this older woman's spirit, and the anointing that's on her life.

What am I to do? Is this truly love, or is it the lonely talking again? I really need to know. But I'm thinking only time spent with her on the outside once I'm out of prison can confirm or deny whether or not these feelings that I have for her to be a reality.

It's amazing how making one decision, which was to write her, while being fully persuaded that nothing related to having personal feelings could ever come out of it, could affect or possibly change your life forever. Could it be that this was in the Lord's plans all along? And would I be rejecting His plans and purpose for my life if I were to choose to stick with my initial plan, which was to marry the younger and more attractive woman of God whom I'm yet to meet?

Sometimes I wish that the Lord would audibly say, "Perry, marry Rosie," or, "It's up to you," or "Don't; I have someone else for you." You see, one of the issues I'm dealing with is that I'm convinced I'll never find another woman like her. Sometimes I even feel that maybe the Lord has already spoken to me loud and clear on this, and maybe my preference or desire for, as they say, "a cutie pie," has caused me to miss God or to give a deaf ear to the voice of God.

The Bible tells us that the steps of a good man are ordered by the Lord, and I'm looking unto the Lord to fulfill His Word in my life concerning her.

The Life of a Song

Isn't it amazing how music can hold time in the palm of its hand? There are literally hundreds of songs that cause my mind to travel back in time, even to the point when I was at the age of ten. Unfortunately this phenomenon seems to take place with or without one's consent.

I'm literally reminded of every relationship I've been involved in over the years, which takes me all the way back to grade school, when I thought a kiss on the cheek was the best thing since getting your first bike for Christmas. Even now, I occasionally listen to a couple of R&B songs off the radio; you know, good clean songs that promote love for a woman.

And every time I hear a familiar song that I used to listen to when I was in various relationships throughout my past, it never ceases to amaze me how I seem to revisit those old feelings I once had for a particular girl during that era.

Even for a split second while listening to that song, it is as though the very pit of my stomach is having a flirting session with the past.

Which leads me to the conclusion that there is life in a song, and it is always saying something.

Therefore, I'm inclined to believe that this type of music is not healthy for the believer. Although it may be lawful to listen to it, and may not be a sin within itself, it could lead you in that direction, especially for the unmarried.

Songs from the past can cause one to reminisce about past relationships, which could reflect images of sexual sins that were once experienced by you and the one whom the song reminds you of. Those same images could possibly follow you to bed and have its way in your sleep. Nothing good can come from that. It could even lead some who aren't as strong as others to be consumed by a spirit of masturbation.

The Bible tells us that life and death are in the power of the tongue, and they that love it shall eat the fruit thereof. That is why the words of a song have a lasting effect. There is power in a spoken word that could influence or shape your future, even if it is in a song. I'm mainly referring to my brothers and sisters who are single and incarcerated. Although songs from the past can affect those who are married and incarcerated in a negative way as well, such as causing or inviting the spirit of loneliness, causing one to become more impatient, stressed, and more prone to giving in to the enemy's devices.

Married couples on the outside, on the other hand, have the luxury of choosing their selection of songs and making them their own, which could remind them of one another for the rest of their lives.

So I encourage every believer to use wisdom before attempting to venture back down memory lane through the vehicle of entertaining songs from the past.

Another Family Crisis

Well, my family has been going back and forth to court trying to get a judge to determine whether my grandfather will continue living with my aunt, who's an evangelist, or if he will decide to honor the request of another aunt of mine and decide or determine that he should move back home so that everyone will have mutual access to him. Personally I feel that this is more about having access to my granddaddy's money than to him.

It's obvious that no one trusts anyone in the family when it comes to money, and unfortunately, for good reason. No one within the family has exemplified a pattern of good money management skills. Although I do feel that the evangelist is not only better suited for the job, but she's also doing a great job with what's most important concerning my granddaddy, and that is attending to his inabilities.

So waking up the day after court was held, the first thing on my mind was to call my younger aunt, who's sort of neutral in the situation, to find out the details and which way the judge ruled. Unfortunately, I was told that the judge had delayed his ruling for another six months.

And to make matters worse, while Aunt Louise was hugging and kissing my granddaddy for a seemingly very long time, as he motioned to pull away, my Uncle Timbo tried to assist him by attempting to pry him away from her, accompanied with a request to let him go. Before he could get "go" out of his mouth, I was told that Aunt Louise had hit him in it, loosening several teeth. Without a moment's notice, Uncle Timbo had responded with a combination of his own, which sent her to the hospital and him to jail.

This happened right outside the courtroom in the presence of law officials who witnessed the incident. So it looks like Aunt Louise will be going to jail as well, once she's released from the hospital.

Now can you get a glimpse of why my granddaddy has had eleven silent strokes in the recent years, and my grandmother suffered from heart trouble before passing away?

Uncle Timbo has had run-ins with the law all of his life, with the exception of the last ten years, which was when he decided to relocate to another state in his pursuit to start a new life away from his family. After making the decision to visit limited family members, it didn't take but two months before finding himself back in a familiar place called the Metro County Jail.

The Bible tells us that a man's enemy shall be those of his own household. Although the Lord Jesus is the dividing factor in this Scripture, we know that Satan divides as well, but for evil.

I'm praying for my uncle, even though it seems as though our past life of drug dealing has sort of driven a wedge between us in the sense that we're not as close as we once were. If he only knew the love I have for him and my intentions of being a blessing to him once I'm released from prison.

I just want to see my family blessed and living the victorious life which the Lord intended for them to live.

I Nearly Lost Him

Well, it was only a few days since the chaotic incident had taken place with my family outside of the courtroom when I thought to call my aunt the evangelist to get her take on what happened. To my surprise, she was at the hospital with my grandfather. He had to be resuscitated; I believe because he had choked on something.

So he immediately had surgery on his throat in order to widen it in an attempt to prevent it from happening again. Ironically this had to happen only a few days after he had witnessed his fifty-plus-year-old children fighting outside the courtroom door.

I tell you, it takes a strong-willed father, determined to live, accompanied by God's grace, to be able to endure and survive the constant violence and drama that has been manifested within the family throughout the years. Being that there's no sign of letting up. I've considered the possible reality that my grandfather may not be around when I get there. So I did the only wise thing a man in my situation could do; I began to pray.

Not long after that, I was led to write a letter to Attorney General Eric Holder to express my concern for my grandfather; the fact that it was going on nine months since last I heard from his office concerning my claim; and to respectfully make it known of my awareness of the possibility of politics wanting to play a role in the process.

Although I know nothing can prevent God's will from being done, and I will be home soon, I still know that Satan will try and use every available resource in his attempt to hinder the Lord's plans. I'm just so thankful God's favor is on my life, and that my destiny is inevitable.

Still, I'm of the opinion that the attorney general has considered whether this could end quietly or not. Could the publicity of the outcome affect the mid-term election for the House and Senate, which takes place in November of this year, being that one of the defendants was appointed by the president himself? Not to mention the fact that the House, the Senate, as well as the president have become very unpopular these days.

So I'm sure the Democrats are trying to avoid or conceal any more stumbling blocks, at least until after the election.

Trying to Get the Speck Out of Her Eye, I Discovered a Plank in Mine

Well, for the first time since the three years that Rosie and I have been a part of each other's lives, we had a disagreement. It came as a shock to me because it has never happened before. Besides that, I didn't see a reason for it.

She had an appointment to see the doctor about her severe back injury that has caused her to endure much pain. About a week before her visit, she gave all the money she had to her son, who obviously had a need as well. Being that I have her best interest at heart, I felt compelled to lovingly disagree with her decision of making such a painful sacrifice.

She defended her decision by telling me that her son has never asked her for anything since moving out and getting married. I then reminded her of other past instances wherein she made sacrifices for her son.

Instead of her understanding the picture I was trying to paint as an attempt to help her become a better steward over her limited finances, she only expressed resentment of always confiding in me about personal matters. Long story short, she later conceded to it being a misunderstanding.

Ironically, after only a few weeks later, I was inspired to bless my mother with a portable speaking Bible, my aunt with a Bible cover, and Rosie with a shoulder bag to carry her books, all of which were warranted and very helpful at the time. Needless to say, after getting a few things for myself, I was left with seventeen cents in my account.

A day later I received an e-mail from my youngest daughter, Kiara, asking me if I could call her. I began to feel a little discouraged, to say the least, being that I had just recently told her that if she ever needed me, that I was just an e-mail away, and that I would come running to her aid.

I asked several counselors if I could make a call; they couldn't. The chaplain wasn't in. I constantly checked my account, hoping that someone may have thought to send me something, or maybe the Lord would supernaturally put just enough in my account to call my baby, all to no avail.

I felt helpless, and more desperate than a pile of overgrown rattlesnakes. Which means I was at the point of almost breaking the rules, something I never do, in order to see what my daughter had wanted with me.

But the Spirit of God wouldn't allow it. Instead He used this opportunity as a teaching tool. One, to help me identify with Rosie's love for her children, and the fact that she'll do anything for them, just as I would for mine. Also, that she still needs to be a better steward over what she has, using wisdom rather than her heart as the motivating factor concerning how she disburses her goods. Only she's not alone in making this adjustment.

After letting my daughter down by not being able to call her to see whether or not she was OK due to trying to play Santa Claus during the month of August, made it apparent that I, too, needed to work on my stewardship ability, especially being that I am expecting great wealth from the Lord through my deliverance from prison. Why would God bless me with millions at a time when I'm unable to manage two hundred dollars a month in prison?

Finally, as I understand my shortcomings and my endeavor to correct them, I feel obligated to share with Rosie the discovery of having to deal with the very thing that I had preached to her about, hoping that my confession won't lead her to feel that her issue is more acceptable and common for Christians rather than desiring to work together to help rid one another of this possible blessing blocker.

Sometimes doing a good thing isn't always the right thing. Prayerfully we will prevail.

A Quest to Prepare an Unprepared Family for Wealth

For me, I know there's a bigger picture. I'm fully persuaded that God has called me to be a millionaire in His Kingdom, which comes with great responsibility. I have a heart to want to bless my family financially. But I'm well aware of their financial incapabilities.

Some have had large sums of money in their possession more than once; others have been blessed with a career-oriented job that pays well; while few have yet to see more than ten thousand dollars at once. Unfortunately, when I try and think of someone to call that could possibly have an extra fifty dollars to send me if I needed it, no one comes to mind. Not that they wouldn't if they had it, but the chances of them having it just isn't good.

As with any family, bad habits as well as bad money management skills are usually the core reason for limited resources. So even though the desire is there to go as far as setting up various businesses for my family to run, or to give them a substantial amount of monies to do with as they please, it would be foolish to do so unless a changed mindset precedes it.

To simply ignore the wisdom of God and allow the love for my family to dictate how I invest the monies that the Lord entrusted me with sets me up for the inevitable. The Bible tells us that a fool and his money are soon parted, which simply means that if I follow a pattern that is contrary to God's recipe for continued success, then I can expect a decrease in my revenue rather than an increase.

It is my intent to help prepare them mentally as well as spiritually for this season of prosperity that is about to take place. But I know that arrogance and attitudes exist in some, which often tends to overcrowd any room, for constructive criticism or an exhortation concerning an effort to overcome weaknesses.

In spite of how it looks, I proclaim that they'll be prepared people who will have positioned themselves to receive the blessings of God and to use them for His glory.

He Keeps Doing Great Things for Me

After several days of torment for not being able to call my daughter, I poured my heart out to God while lying in bed at around midnight, asking for His mercy, assuring Him that I've learned much from this experience, praying that all would be well once I've contacted my daughter, and to touch someone's heart to send me some money so that I could call her. I couldn't wait to sleep the night away in order to see what another day would bring.

Embracing the sound of the alarm coming from my wristwatch confirming that it was six o'clock in the morning, I made my bed, freshened up, and headed to the computer to see if any money had arrived. I was overwhelmed to find that there was $1520.00 in my account, along with two e-mails! Fifteen hundred dollars had come from the bar association. They had refunded the down payment that I had given to a lawyer who had treated me unfairly over three years ago. First of all, getting money back from a lawyer while in prison is very slim, to say the least. But the timing of it signified that it was of the Lord.

The other twenty dollars was from my daughter Kiara. I made a desperate attempt to try and call her collect—something that I had never done before. Although she was unable to accept it, she knew that it was me, and figured that I didn't have any money, then did something which she had never done before. She sent me twenty dollars, which was her last, and hoped that it would help me, which she had stated in one of the two e-mails, which was sent by her as well.

So now I'm seeing the power of God at work: the love of my youngest daughter for her father; and a slight feeling of embarrassment as well as great gratitude on my part, due to the fact that I've never received any money from my daughter before, which also illuminated the possibility that there may be some hidden pride in that area of my life that needs to be dealt with. It has always been difficult for me to ask anyone for money, so for me to ask my children made it much harder.

After calling and thanking her for giving me all she had, I was able to minister to her the principle of sowing and reaping. Once I felt she had an understanding of it, I was thrilled to tell her that I was blessed with some more money from another source, and that I was sending her one hundred dollars. That one instance not only enabled me to teach her the benefits in giving, but the Lord also graced her with the actual experience of receiving the benefit of it all at once.

The Lord also took the sting out of the apparent pride of not wanting to receive money from my daughter by blessing me with the money to reward her for her unselfish giving. Who would dare argue the greatness of my God?

10
Feeling Good About Knowing That Something Is About to Happen While Preparing for the Same

Well, it's been a couple of weeks now, and it seems like a good day to write. Today's date is 10/10/10, and I'm just so excited with the reality of this being my season. And I sense in my spirit that I may be home by Christmas. Even the mere possibility of being home for Christmas just makes me want to shout those three famous words: Ho! Ho! Ho!

I know that being home for such a memorable occasion as Christmas would cause me to be looked upon by many as a type of Santa Claus by those who love me and have long awaited for this moment to arrive. One couldn't ask for a better gift that brings joy to all those who are in the house, including the gift itself.

Going home has become such a reality within my spirit, so much so that it became natural for me to quit my job that pays me two hundred dollars a month in order to better prepare myself mentally as well as spiritually to be transitioned back into society, where I will be totally dependent on the Lord in every area of my life.

Two hundred dollars a month is a lot of money to forfeit in prison, but a small sacrifice to make for serenity. Besides, working in the UNICOR factory here is a real distraction. All of the government officials lack integrity and they lie for the fun of it. They don't even care if they're exposed to be the liars that they are. It's as though they're saying, "You need this job too bad. You know it, and we know it. So get back to work." From the warden on down to the COs, about 95% are deceivers. It's hard to conceive how they all can have the same thing in common. It's as though being a good liar was one of the requirements for getting hired.

This kind of character flaw is not limited to only those government officials that are over UNICOR. This type of mentality is filtrated throughout every department within the prison, especially in medical.

My Christian brother and close friend named Harold, who I spoke about earlier, is one of many men that have been deprived of proper medial attention. Some have even lost their life because of it. Brother Harold continuously complained about the pain in his stomach, only to be treated for constipation. After many months of no relief, he finally convinced staff to give him a colonoscopy, which revealed that he had cancer.

Months after being accurately diagnosed, he was taken to a medical facility for treatment. I'm standing on the Word of God that he shall live and not die. But his condition could have been treated much sooner had they been more concerned about his well-being instead of the cost of the necessary procedures that this type of illness called for.

We were just given the privilege of having a black warden around the beginning of this year. There were a couple of things that he had done on the behalf of the inmate population that's worth mentioning. One of the first things he had done was cancel the Martin Luther King holiday meal; and the other was to cancel the black history month celebration. He set the tone right away by making it known that he just looks relatable. No one was looking for special favors—only fairness—but none could be found.

I could touch on every department and give an example of the oppressive spirit that resides within the institution, but I think that I've made my point. It's apparent that this branch of government has no interest or endeavor to invest a certain level of integrity and moral excellence in the lives of the inmates here in prison, which would afford them a much better chance of surviving and making a positive impact in society and in the lives of their family.

If those who are in authority over us don't possess the very attributes that those who are incarcerated desperately need, apart from God, where does the motivation for rehabilitation come from?

Yeah, I agree that it should be incumbent upon every man to at least desire to want to change after experiencing the loss of freedom, family, and all that comes with it. But who needs the distractions from the frustration of staff members, who are transparent when it comes to revealing their true identity and feelings toward your well-being? Simply put, they could care less one way or the other.

Should Christians Cooperate with the Government for the Purpose of a Sentence Reduction?

Well, I've been at this institution for several years now, and I've seen men go back and forth to court for the purpose of testifying against others in exchange for a sentence reduction, some of whom are professed Christians. The question is rather or not this kind of conduct is acceptable in the eyes of God.

Let's begin with those who aren't saved. Although God loves them as much as He loves those who are saved, apart from surrendering their lives to Him, there's nothing that they can do in and of themselves to please God. So when we attempt to look through the eyes of the unsaved, we see that he's accountable to only one person—himself. Which means about 98 percent of the time self-preservation will dictate the decision to testify against another for a lighter sentence.

The alternative is to remain true to the code of ethics which was established long ago by criminals of ancient history. If you can't do the time, then don't do the crime; or death before dishonor; just to name a couple of slogans that simply mean that if you get caught, keep your mouth shut.

This is a rule that's commonly known by the average person who decides to break the law. But when a person is faced with the reality of going to prison for decades or possibly for the rest of their life, the option to bear the shame of as the streets call it, "snitch," becomes as easy as singing a song in the shower. This has been going on for so long and now more frequently than ever, until selling drugs has become a fool's game.

This has become an epidemic that has plagued the black community for nearly twenty-five years. It has destroyed homes, families, and communities across the United States. Parents go to prison for an unjustifiable length of time, only to leave their children victimized, destined to follow in their parents' footsteps due to the void of structure in the home throughout their adolescent life. In this rare occasion, it's obvious that the real criminal is the system that governs, prosecutes, and sentences criminals to an unprecedented amount of time for a nonviolent offense. I'll be the first to say that we should be punished for breaking the law; but in this case, the crime just doesn't fit the time.

Now concerning those who are saved and later decide to go back to court and testify against someone in exchange for a sentence reduction, is God pleased with that? I would have to say no, He's not. There are times when believers are young in the faith and could be what the Bible calls "carnal" Christians, which are simply immature Christians. Being that they're weak in the faith, their desire to go home supersedes the desire to want to please the Lord.

That is why there should be accountability within the Christian body, and those who are spiritually mature should take the time to counsel the younger believer and show them a more excellent way in the Lord. The bearing of our own pain of being in prison away from our loved ones is a testament that the person you will potentially testify against will experience the same pain or worse. The Bible tells us to love your neighbor as yourself; therefore we shouldn't subject anyone to something that we ourselves wouldn't want to go through.

Then there's the "do unto others as you would have them to do unto you" principle, and I don't believe that anyone can consciously say that they would want someone to help incarcerate them for any length of time, especially under the federal system.

We should always seek to have the mindset of our Lord and Savior, Jesus Christ. We deserved justice, which was eternal death, for our sins. Instead He chose to give us mercy, which was eternal life, by taking our place and dying on the cross in our stead. Love will always lead us to mercy and sacrifice rather than justice and self-preservation.

Now should a Christian accept responsibility and plead guilty if he's guilty? In my opinion, being that the sentencing guidelines are so unfair, although they are in the process of changing that, still I would prayerfully instruct my attorney to get the best deal possible, while asking God to let the sentence come from Him. The Bible tells us that the king's heart is in the hands of the Lord, and as the rivers of water, He turns it whichever way He wills (Proverbs 21:1).

So I believe that we can take heart in the fact that God is sovereign, and nothing happens except He allows it. Therefore I believe choosing to go down this path and not testifying against another would be the choice that a man of God should take.

The only other option would be to go to trial, which only gives you about a two percent chance of winning, being that a conspiracy charge was constructed in such a way whereas false testimonies can get you up to a life sentence. And false testimonies are more likely to be included in your case than not, being that the average person is desperate to go home.

Besides that, I've learned through experience that prosecutors willingly use, even coerce, witnesses to make false statements. Most importantly, even if you had a better chance of winning than two percent, if you're guilty of the charge, you will have to win it on your own.

The God I serve will not influence, back, or fight for a lie; and much prayer and fasting won't change His nature. He's the God of truth, so for us to ask Him to deliver us in this way is just like asking Him to stop being God. He longs to step in and assist us, but He's looking for transparency, a heart of repentance, humility, and a cry for mercy. This will create an atmosphere that warrants a divine sentence from the Lord, accompanied with His peace and strength to bear it.

Seize Every Moment Given by Your Children to Tell Them About God's Goodness and Their Need for Him

Speaking with my youngest daughter just the other day, I found her to be perplexed about an apparent character flaw which she admitted to having, yet found it overwhelmingly difficult to overcome. She said that everyone tells her that she has an attitude problem. And although she has accepted that as a reality, no matter how hard she tries to control it, she fails miserably.

Before responding, I knew this to be what the Bible calls a generational curse, something that she inherited from her mother who also inherited from her mother. I understood that this wouldn't be easy for her to understand, especially without the Holy Spirit living inside her in order to reveal this spiritual truth to her, realizing that the greatest teacher whoever lived was our Lord and Savior, Jesus Christ, who was always methodical in His teaching by using everyday life experiences, circumstances, and surroundings in order to make spiritual truths understandable to the natural man.

At the risk of appearing to her as a villain in my past life, I ventured out to give her a couple of examples from my past life and a little from her mother's as well. I began by telling her something she already knew, which was the fact that her mother as well as her grandmother shared the same attitude problem as she does.

Then I began telling her something that was rather challenging for me to say: the fact that I was whorish all of my life, as was my father and grandfather. I shared with her that after going to state prison for the second time, I gave my life to the Lord for the first time. It was there where I married her mother. Once I got out of prison, I was a young Christian having been saved for about fourteen months. However, I was determined to be faithful to the Lord and her mother as well.

After being tested on several occasions by turning down invites of girls from past relationships, for the very first time in life I realized that I had overcome the power and influence of whoredom that had dogged me all of my life. But it wasn't me that had overcome it; it was the power of the Holy Spirit that had control of my life.

Before I continued, I made it known to her that I was about to say something concerning her mother that had no bearing on the woman she is today, and that this is only for her learning, and she should always see her mother for the queen she is. Past mistakes should never define or alter one's perception of the present.

I went on to tell her that her mother was dissatisfied with my present income that I was making when I first got out of prison and suggested that I go back to my old occupation of making fast money the illegal way. After constant complaints and infidelity on her part, we had separated more than once, only to get back together again.

Me being a Christian for such a short time, I fell subject to the silent ultimatum that was echoing in my own mind: Either I'm going to let my wife go and please the Lord, or let the Lord go and please my wife. I responded as a foolish man by choosing the latter.

Unfortunately, as a dog returning to his vomit, not only did I go back to selling drugs, but having affairs with other women as well.

So I told her all of this to show her that I enjoyed the freedom over the power and persuasion of women for just this brief moment in my life due to the saving power of my Lord and Savior, Jesus Christ. Likewise, I made it known to her that the Lord is the answer to any and every problem that is too big for us to solve. He is the solution to our sin problem. From her attitude problem to my infidelity, He's the only cure.

Did God Make Us This Way?

One may wonder, why am I like this? Plagued with various inherited character defects that control my life with or without my consent, did God make me this way?

That is a good question. People have been blaming God and lying on Him since the beginning of mankind. Some say, "It's not my fault that I have homosexual tendencies, an attitude problem, or the spirit of a fornicator on my life, etc. If I was born with it, then I shouldn't be held accountable for it."

Not that God needs any defending, but the Bible clearly states that God made man in His image and in His likeness. Being that we know that God is without sin, then it would be safe to say that He is vindicated of the claim of having anything to do with us being fallible and imperfect creatures.

No, our problem came when the first man, Adam, stepped out of the will of God and disobeyed the one and only commandment that he was given, which was, "Do not eat of the tree of knowledge of good and evil." That was when sin had passed down to every man, for all men had sinned in Adam.

So when we acknowledge that we have this sin problem and understand where it came from, as well as admitting that we can't fix it ourselves, our only questions should be, are we going to live with it and suffer the eternal consequences that come with it, or do we go back to the Creator of us all, who has the antidote to our sin sickness?

Any time we as rational people purchase an appliance of some sort with a warranty, as soon as it is broken, common sense tells us to take it back to the manufacturer before the warranty expires. The same principle applies spiritually, when we come to understand that our very being is in jeopardy of spending eternity in hell unless we return back to our Maker in order to be renewed or remanufactured before life's warranty expires. The latter choice should be rational and common sense as well.

Who's the Mother?

Thinking of my mother, I decided to call and see how she was doing, as I often do. As you know, she's been living with my sister for several years now, in which I'm very grateful for. Anyway, my sister answered the phone and shared with me some information that I wasn't aware of. My mother had been seeing this man for a short period of time, and because of his apparent excessive drinking problem, my sister suddenly disapproves of the relationship.

Although I agree with her, especially being that our mother has had a drinking problem for many years prior to moving in with her, what I don't agree with is the fact that my sister being in disagreement with anything pertaining to our mother is defined as null and void. Simply put, what she says goes, end of story.

Now I know this all sounds unusual, and that it's normally the other way around, but it's obvious that you don't know my sister. She's a good person, but at the same time she's pretty aggressive and forceful in communicating with others, especially when it's contrary to her way of thinking.

My sister grew up playing sports and fighting, a combination that's destined to rear a person up to be tough, to say the least, unlike myself. I grew up on the cool side, chasing young girls and avoiding fighting by any means necessary.

I remember when we were in grade school, there was this notorious family known for bullying and fighting. For some unknown reason, I found myself right smack in the middle of my worst nightmare. As soon as we had gotten off the school bus, I saw my sister flying through the air, diving across the back of one of the members of this family who fought for the fun of it. She and my youngest uncle were feuding with them without my knowledge.

So here I am standing on the sidelines watching what I call a horror movie, wondering whether or not someone is going to swing and hit me and force me into my very first fight, in which I'm sure to lose, being that the opponents were like professionals to me. Fortunately it never happened, and my first fight didn't come until middle school.

Now I know what you're thinking; how could I stand there and watch my family go to battle and do nothing? Simple. I was only eight years old; and besides that, I was petrified. And if that's not enough, it just wasn't in my DNA. Ironically, the baddest and oldest brother in that family became one of my closest friends as we grew older. But back to the matter at hand. That was just one of many examples which helped to shape and mold my sister into the woman that she is today.

So although my mother desired to voice her opinion and to make her own decision in this matter, she dare not say a word. Even though I try to avoid having conversations with my sister that I know will bring out the aggression that I'm believing God to deliver her from, helping her to see what's best for our mother is always a warranted reason. No one should be deprived of the privilege to exercise the liberty of having some input in making decisions that could affect their lives, for better or worse, as an adult.

Although my sister's judgment seems to be more sound, the respectful thing should be to convey your advice to that someone in love, with the understanding that the ultimate decision is in their hands. That tends to keep things in perspective, while allowing both parties to embrace a sense of relevancy and self-worth.

So I thought it to be wise to simply write my sister a letter to assure myself that there would be no interruptions until all was said and that time was given in order for her to consider our mother's position as well as mindset, in which my sister may be potentially unaware of. Afterwards, my intentions are to call her and to hear her response to the matter. Hopefully it will be a peaceful one.

My Sister's Response

Well, it's Sunday night, which is the night I usually call to talk with my mother and sister. As the phone began to ring, my sister answered by saying, "What's up, gal?" She's been playing with me for years now, addressing me as her sister; and although she's well aware of the fact that I'm unappreciative of her joking with me in that manner, I can tell that she has no intentions on stopping any time in the near future.

So as we began to talk, I asked her if she received my letter. She immediately responded by saying, "Boy, I ain't thinking about you." Then in her next statement, she told me that our mother stayed the weekend with our aunt, and they went fishing.

Now fishing to my mother is the next best thing to her son coming home from prison. Fishing has always been her first love, so letting her go fishing in the same week that she received my letter was my sister's way of saying she agrees with me, and that she would allow our mother to have more liberty when it comes to her own life.

So that was a victory, particularly for my mother. But I'm believing that this will begin to bring a sense of sensitivity within my sister concerning life's issues as it pertains to others.

People come from various places mentally and emotionally. Life's trials and struggles have shaped some to be tough as nails, while others to be soft as drugstore cotton. Both personalities can be used to do great things in life, especially in the hands and under the influence of the Creator. But neither should place a burden on the other with the expectation of walking in their shoes, which were uniquely designed for their feet, and theirs alone.

11
Twelve Days Before Christmas

Well, it's twelve days till Christmas, and ever since I've been incarcerated, I've yet to miss a year of sending out Christmas cards, and even gifts to loved ones. That is, up until now. I am literally in the spirit of living moment by moment as it pertains to my deliverance. I may or may not be in prison on Christmas day, but the pull of my deliverance is so strong right now until it's as if I've been confined to the now.

Every day I awake, I anticipate my name being called, verifying my release. So for me to purchase gifts ahead of time to send to my family, making sure they get them before Christmas, just feels weird to me, and contradicts the very state of my present being.

Some may think this is some religious exercise or mind over matter tactic that I'm attempting. But if truth were to speak without a mouthpiece, I believe that He would exonerate me of having anything to do with manufacturing or dictating this awesome place that I've found myself to be in.

The Bible tells us that the blessings of the Lord maketh one rich and addeth no sorrow with it. God didn't tell me that I would or wouldn't be home for Christmas. But I'm fully persuaded that He has given me a mandate to be ready, because it could be any moment now. So whether I'm there by December the 25th or not, I'm going to praise my God regardless, with the anticipation that I could be there in a moment's notice.

It's amazing that my best friend and Spirit-filled sister, Rosie, told me before I was able to tell her, that we're not going to send each other gifts this year, and that whether I make it home for Christmas or not, there will be no regrets. The Lord really blessed me when He brought her into my life. He even used her to break that superficial necessity of having to have a cutie pie for a wife.

I have so much love for her, and even though it may not be God's intended purpose for her to be my wife, He has really used her in sculpting the man of God that I'm becoming. Although time holds the key in revealing whether or not she will be my wife, I'm just so satisfied in knowing that she's my friend.

Identifying the Marks for the Making of God's Set Man

In preparing for a ministry that God has called you to while in prison, you begin to realize that about nine out of ten men that have been saved for a while and have learned a fairly substantial amount of knowledge from the Word of God seem to feel that they belong behind a pulpit and/or leading God's people. I believe that to be largely so, as a direct result of our past life prior to knowing the Lord.

Whether we were dealing in drugs or robbers, etc., we had some form of control and loved it. Now that we've become citizens of God's Kingdom, we tend to bring those same flawed characteristics with us. And in doing so, our ego and pride are easily flared up when opposition gets in the way of our destination, which is to ultimately run something or someone.

Although this kind of problem is prevalent within the body in the prison system, I find it to be present in the church on the outside as well. There are so many ministers residing over God's people before their time that have not been prepared or sent by God. As the saying goes, "Some were sent; others just went."

But in keeping with my thought as it pertains to identifying God's set man, I've witnessed men in prison that have been saved fifteen to twenty years and well-versed in the Word of God with the gift to teach and preach His Word, but have found themselves to be in rage and ready to fight another brother when they sense what is perceived to be their authority or position has been challenged or threatened.

The Bible tells us that our gift will make room for us. Therefore we need not fight in order to keep it. But if God hasn't put you there and your pride and ambition have, there will continue to be contentions and struggles to try and hold on to something that was never given to you by God Himself.

The Bible also tells us in the book of Proverbs that before honor comes humility. So if a man doesn't possess the markings of humility coupled with love, even though the knowledge and gift which he operates in may be remarkable, he does not qualify to be God's set man. We see glimpses of these two character traits in men chosen by God to serve and shepherd His people.

Abraham is the father of faith, and was given unbelievable promises from God, but he still listened to his wife regarding what must have been a hard decision to send his son, Ishmael, and his mother away that God's will would be done; even to allow his nephew Lot to choose the portion of land that he desired and leaving himself with the lesser.

Joseph was shown dreams of being a ruler, yet after being sold into slavery by his brothers and falsely accused by Potiphar's wife, which landed him in prison for years, once the dream was fulfilled, instead of seeking revenge, he showed love towards them.

Moses led hundreds of thousands of God's people out of Egypt, and even though many of them came up against him on numerous occasions, he never ceased to intercede on their behalf, that God wouldn't take their lives; even in heeding the advice of his father-in-law, Jethro, for him to choose able men that fear God, men of truth and haters of covetousness, to help minister to the people in order to prevent himself from being worn out. Moses was considered to be the most humble man to ever live apart from our Lord and Savior, Jesus Christ.

David killed lions and bears in order to protect his father's herd, and didn't tell a soul until it was needed to be told as a résumé, in order to be chosen to defeat Goliath. King Saul eventually tried to kill him; so did his son, Absalom. Although he was given the opportunity, he never sought revenge. He was called a man after God's own heart by the Lord Himself.

I can go on throughout the Bible in making the case for distinguishing a set man of God, but I think you get my point, and it's my prayer that you will agree. So whether a man desires to be used by God in a small or great way, he must first humble himself and learn to walk in the *agape* love of God before he's able to represent and minister the interests of God concerning His people.

A man who runs to the pulpit is an indication that he seeks to promote himself and to seek the praise of men concerning his gift, rather than to glorify God and to edify His people. On the contrary; a man of God who is mature in love and humility, even though he's aware of his calling to minister, finds contentment in sitting among God's people while someone else ministers. His only concern is that God's people are being properly fed with truth for the edifying of their souls, and that God is being glorified.

When you find this kind of man with these marks, receive him with honor. He's either God's set man in the making, or he's God's made set man.

Suicide Watch

Well, it's four o'clock in the morning, and my sleep was interrupted by the CO. When he stepped in the doorway of my cell and called my name, I immediately assumed, or considered, for lack of a better word, that this could be it—my time to go home. But as he continued to speak, I realized that it wasn't. He asked me to get ready to do suicide watch.

I've been a member of an inmate companion program for a couple of years now. Unfortunately there are times when the trials and pressures of life that come with being incarcerated tend to overwhelm some in such a way that life feels hopeless for them, and the enemy convinces them that their only way of escape or relief is death. I'm thankful that there have only been a few guys that I along with other members of the program have had to sit and watch and attempt to minister hope into their situation.

On this particular occasion, I was surprised to discover after arriving to medical that the man I would be trying to help was someone that I know very well. We call him Blue because of his very dark complexion. He's a muscular man in his mid-forties, and although he professes to be a Christian, the eighteen-plus years he's been incarcerated for a crime that the government is aware that he didn't do has plagued him with nothing but anger and bitterness.

You're probably thinking that the average person in prison claims that he's innocent. I simply disagree. Many of us do have a legitimate claim that the punishment doesn't fit the crime; and even though there are some that are guilty and who will cry innocent until their dying day, there's no doubt in my mind that this man isn't one of them. But because the system is so flawed and void of a safety net to counter the injustice within the government employees who swore to uphold the law, many have become victimized by the system without a voice to speak out on their behalf.

But after talking and praying with him and sharing my testimony, he not only became courageous and empowered by God to get off of suicide watch, but he has also agreed to write a book in order to tell his story as well.

I thank God for the other brothers who allowed the Lord to use them in helping minister to Brother Blue. We all have a story to tell that could penetrate the hearts and minds of others who very well may be going through similar circumstances. Until the Lord provides us with a voice on the outside, let us begin using our own.

Unaltered Faith

Well, Christmas has come and gone, and here I am still in prison, three days into the new year of 2011. Nothing has changed; my faith concerning what God spoke concerning my release remains steadfast and unmovable.

After calling my family on Christmas day to share with them the recognition of Jesus' birth, I was told by one of my aunts that they had reserved two hotels not far from the prison, and they had planned on coming up here to surprise me. I thought that was a wonderful gesture. But being aware of the reason behind them making this sacrifice during the holiday season, which was simply because they were concerned that maybe my faith of coming home soon had been diminished, I insisted that they didn't come. I then began to encourage them and reaffirm to them the *rhema* Word of God that would surely come to pass in this season concerning my deliverance as well as prosperity.

One of the most powerful forces on earth is the spoken Word of God in the life of a believer who would believe it. Regardless of how much time has elapsed and the many trials and tribulations that come up against you, continue to speak it, believe it, and hold fast to what's yours at all cost.

I'm reminded of about fifteen years ago when I had just pulled up to my mother-in-law's house who had owned this vicious dog that had bitten more than a few people and should have been put to death a long time ago. Although he was feared by many, I never liked dogs, and the fear that I had of him far exceeded them all quietly kept.

Anyway, as I was getting out of my car, there were about five children running from around the house, followed by the dog from hell. I wanted to run as well, but two of those children happened to belong to me. So my daughter, who was about six years old at the time, ran and dove into my arms. I instinctively rushed to put her in the car. Before I could shut the door, my ten-year-old son was lying on the ground being attacked by this demon-possessed dog. I was literally numb to the fear that was once a reality in my life prior to the previous fifteen to twenty seconds.

As I raced towards my son to save and protect him from this dog, I nearly broke my foot kicking him in the head. The dog ran back around the house, hollering the whole way there. My son is my seed and I was willing to protect him at all cost.

Likewise, God's Word is identified as a seed, and once you have possession of it, it has to be nurtured and protected from every storm of life or vicious dog that Satan sends to project fear and doubt in you in his attempt to nullify the Word of God. If no one else believes it, you continue to say it and believe it until it manifests.

The Will to Live

Well, I called my aunt, the evangelist, and as you've probably learned by now, there's always some sort of drama going on within the family. Sadly, on this particular occasion, she was at the hospital with my grandfather. He had caught pneumonia and was hooked to the breathing machine because both of his lungs were inoperative, and the doctors had asked that the family be called in because he wasn't expected to make it through the night.

As you know, my grandparents raised me and I had lost my grandmother during my incarceration. But I had asked the Lord for some time with my grandfather on the outside before He calls him home. Besides that, Daddy, which is what I call him, assured me that he'd be there when I got there.

Days later, his will to live, along with my plea to God, began to take precedence over the doctors' prediction. The Great Physician and God of the living proclaimed that my soon to be ninety-five-year-old grandfather shall live and not die. It's amazing how when God does the miraculous, it's not considered or honored among all of those who are affected by it.

After calling for the third or fourth time just to touch base, unfortunately I was not shocked to hear that Aunt Louise had visited Daddy while my other aunt, the evangelist, was still there—a disaster waiting to happen.

As I was told, Aunt Louise, after staring the evangelist down for about thirty seconds, began taking off her shoes to use as a weapon against her. I'm not going any further with the details; I'm sure that you can draw your own conclusions. But I'm just saddened by the control that this spirit has on my family, although I know that he has to take his paws off of them when the priest gets there. But until I do, continued warfare in the spirit will not cease until peace and order is restored. But I'm persuaded and grateful for the Lord's grace and mercy that's keeping and sustaining my daddy while he's forced to witness this persistent madness that's being manipulated by the enemy.

I Give

I'd like for my readers to feel privileged in knowing that you are the first to hear of my decision to marry Rosie. I guess one of my reasons for confiding in you first is because I'm really not looking for any feedback at this time, but to address what I perceive will be some of your thoughts or opinions on the matter.

No, it's not emotionalism or vulnerability. Yes, I know that I said that I'm used to younger and more attractive women, and I know the world is full of them. But I'm persuaded that God's will is for me to marry her. I know now why I'm so attracted to her spirit; it's because hers is so much like my own. And I know that since the beginning I've rejected the notion of us ever becoming husband and wife for no other reason than her appearance, knowing that one of the easiest things in the world would be for me to marry a young and attractive woman of God, while selfishly ignoring the glory that God would receive from choosing His daughter, Rosie, one that I've witnessed firsthand her labor of love and holiness while going through years of trials and hardship, only to be found faithful in the sight of God.

Sometimes I think selfishly and feel that I deserve someone who caters more to my fleshly desires. But the truth of the matter is, I'm undeserving of this anointed, powerful, loving, and totally surrendered woman of God who expresses a picture of God's own heart in all that she does.

Now I find myself often asking God to lighten up on these constant visions of us being together. Not only during the day do I see us together in a beautiful way, but sometimes she interrupts my sleep about 2:00 or 3:00 a.m. with nonstop visions of how our life together would be.

I know that God sometimes reveals His plans for your life in part. When He revealed to me my deliverance, I had no idea that she was a part of it. Not only helping to prepare me for it, but to share in it with me as my wife.

The Bible tells us that a man's steps are of the Lord; how then can a man understand his own way? I would have never seen any of this coming, but that's just like God to shield from you that which you're not ready for or unable to receive.

As a young Christian, I would have surely rejected His plan for my life and would have associated it as being a plan of the enemy. Now it seems as though the Lord is allowing me to see her through His eyes, and she's so beautiful.

I'm often reminded of when we first began talking on the phone; she wanted to know how much time I was given for my alleged crime. My response was, "Just know that I'll be home soon." Although I believed that with all of my heart, I refused to inform her that I was given two consecutive life sentences without the possibility of parole, mainly because I didn't want any pity or doubt from her concerning my situation, even though I perceived her to be a great woman of faith.

But she eventually found out about my sentence, and to my amazement, her response was that she wanted to help increase my faith and prepare me for what God was about to do on my behalf.

I had never witnessed such great faith in a person in reference to someone else's affairs in whom they hardly knew, without even knowing the particulars of that person's problems. But that's the beauty of the God kind of faith; it's not fixed on how big the problem is. Instead it is focused on how big and great our God is.

Until this day, she has not ceased to proclaim and expect to see the manifestation of not only my deliverance, but lives being changed as a result of the testimony that God has given me.

This was just the beginning, and one of many, many examples of how awesome this woman of God is and what she has meant to my life in over the past three years. Besides that, faithfulness, loyalty, and love demonstrated are rarely seen in this kind of environment. Anyone walking in the personification of these characteristics should be esteemed with the highest of honors.

The most inconceivable and God-related element of my decision is the fact that I've never even seen this woman in person other than speaking to her from across the visiting room about eight years ago when she wasn't even a thought in my mind. At this point, she's not even aware of my decision to marry her; neither will she be until I see her on the outside face-to-face for the very first time.

He's with the Lord Now

It's Sunday night. Time to check in with my mother to see how she's doing. After my sister answered the phone with a trembling in her voice, she asked if I had spoken with our aunt the evangelist. In that moment, it was as though time stood still. I made it easier for her by calmly stating that, "Daddy is with the Lord, isn't he?"

Even though I had just lost the one who raised me, the one who is considered to be my twin not only in appearance, but in character as well, God's grace enabled me to go into minister mode where I was able to help uplift and encourage the family as opposed to having an emotional meltdown, which would have made it much more difficult for the family to bear.

It's ironic how I've longed to see my daddy on the outside, embracing the opportunity of showing my appreciation by honoring him for all that he's done for me throughout my life, as only a father could do. But when I think about the fact that he no longer has to witness and endure the torture and disappointment of seeing his children express their rare level of hatred towards one another, I began to think that maybe it is selfish of me to try and hold him here, knowing that God has so much more in store for him than I could ever offer.

But I miss you, Daddy, and I never told you how grateful I am for all that you've sacrificed in raising me from birth, even though you were helpless and unable to accomplish what I believe was one of your most treasured endeavors, which was to see all of your children walking in love and prospering together as a family should.

But I'm willing to accept the responsibility of allowing the Lord to use me in making your heart's desire a living reality. So when I see you in the Lord's Kingdom some day, I'll be able to tell you the awesome news concerning the transformation of your children and the fulfillment of your dream. I'll see you in eternity, Daddy. Love you.

12
Last Letter to Family Before Coming Home

After acknowledging my granddaddy's death and the declaration that I made in dedication of what he has meant to me, to allow the Lord to use me to speak life into my family, I was reminded of Ezekiel's experience when the Lord showed him a vision of a valley of dry bones, then asked him a question, "Can these bones live?" Then the Lord told him to prophesy upon these bones and say unto them, "O ye dry bones, hear the Word of the Lord. I will cause breath to enter into you, and ye shall live."

There was no way Ezekiel could have caused those bones to live without the manifested power of the living God. Neither can I speak life into the calloused hearts of my family without God's presence and power actively being in operation in the tumultuous task that is set before me.

I've attempted to bring my family together before by writing what I thought was a heartfelt letter surely to bring about unity within the family, and mailed a copy to every household, but to no avail. Well, at least until about six months later when my youngest aunt made peace with everyone. That alone made the letter, along with my prayers, a success, but still there's a long way to go.

I believe the root of my family's problem, other than not knowing the Lord, stems from their love of money and stress over not having any due to their bad habits and lack of good money management skills. So I was led to write the family another letter, but instead of addressing their love problem, I touched on what I believe to be the driving force behind the lack of love and unity within the family. Being that I share everything with you, this is what I said to them.

Final Letter Before Coming Home

Hello, family. I thought I'd write this last letter to you while we're recovering from the loss of our Daddy. It's very rare that I'm able to talk with you all when your hearts are sensitive and receptive to change for the good of everyone, if ever. And even though this may not be an exception, I felt the need to make an attempt.

We're all sorrowful and will miss Daddy dearly, but it would be selfish of us to want to keep him here longer than God intended for him to stay, especially when we had nothing more to give him as a family but disappointment and misery.

Without even bringing God into the equation, it's obvious that we love money more than we do one another. I'm not out there with you yet; still, I've been affected by the family's greed.

In the twelve and a half years that I've been here, I was often aware of many occasions when people outside of the family would give those within the family money to send me, only I never got it. It's one thing that your money management skills are so lousy that you couldn't send me money even if you wanted to. But when you don't possess the honor or integrity to allow someone else to receive a thank you letter from me because you found something else to do with my money, shows the condition of your heart.

It doesn't matter how you try to justify it. I can care less about the money. My concern is that one day you'll get sick of yourselves and want to be better. We're supposed to be setting aside an inheritance for our grandchildren instead of a pile of debt.

I'm on my way home. No longer will I ask you to learn to love each other. That's between you and God. If I owe you anything, the first thing that I'm going to do is pay you. Other than that, I'm not giving my money away to people with holes in their pockets. But if any of you want to get out of debt and learn to invest your money, I'll be there for you.

As much as I'd like to see my family experience all that God has in store for them in this life and the next, them failing to do so will not keep me from living the quality of life that the Lord has destined for me to live.

Last Letter to Family Before Coming Home

Know that I love you all, but I'm going on in the plans and purposes of God without looking back. So I hope to see you all by my side.

Love, Perry!

Some may feel that I may have been a little too hard on them, especially during a time when we've just lost our grandfather. But I beg to differ. You all have witnessed countless times when my family has demonstrated a pattern of insensitivity in their actions or reactions concerning a matter. Therefore, their past testifies against them in saying that they don't respond well to soft words and fair speeches. This is a prime example where tough love is a necessity.

Because I'm a soft-spoken man, it grieves me to be compelled in having to speak with my loved ones in this way. But love demands this, and time is of the essence. Satan is not going to ease up regarding his endeavor to destroy my family, and neither is God with His aggressive approach, laced with love, to snatch them out of the kingdom of darkness that they may be productive citizens in the Kingdom of His dear Son.

So the foundation has been set and I'm hopeful that there's an understanding between us of what is expected upon my arrival. I'm sincerely anticipating amazing things to come forth and to be continued throughout this side of heaven as it pertains to my family.

Town News

As I stated recently, I've been privy to reading the newspaper from my hometown for quite a while now, although I was reluctant to reading it in the beginning, thinking it would be a waste of my time; something I hate doing. Nevertheless, it was beneficial for me that I did. For in the confines of those papers is where God unveiled a vast portion of those who would be affected by my ministry.

I've consistently read about kids, mainly from the ages of sixteen to twenty years of age, whom Satan has beguiled and succeeded in them partaking in the spirit of murder, usually capital murder, which carries the death penalty. And when I look at their picture in the paper, their eyes tell the whole story with just a few words: "How did I get here?"

As I read their minds, mine is screaming the answer: "I'm to blame!" Myself, along with many other fathers that are in prison who left their children behind with nothing but a roadmap to follow that simply says, "This is what I've done, son. Now you try and top it."

The saddest thing is that Satan has raised the bar. Instead of putting drugs in their hands with the intentions of making money without any casualties, he now puts an automatic weapon in their hands with instructions to go and take what you want, and afterwards, pull the trigger.

My brother and cellmate believes that God is raising up an army from behind prison walls that are willing to sacrifice their life in an effort to save our children. I concur. I see the mind of God in this matter; to prepare a people that came from the streets and who contributed to the condition of our children by their past life. I became acclimated on this divine mission through a dream that God gave me.

My wife and I were leaving the house. I don't remember who she was, so that wasn't to my knowledge a significant factor other than the fact that I would have a wife. Anyway, as we were driving through the neighborhood at a slow pace, a young man with a pistol in his hand approached me and demanded money.

As I stopped the car and began reaching for my wallet, I was led to begin witnessing to him, letting him know that I was a minister and that it was my desire to help him.

I told him that this little money that I'm giving him won't last, and he'll soon have to do it again. But I asked him to afford me the opportunity of talking with him on tomorrow about surviving and providing for his family without ever having to do this again.

I then told him that God loved him and has a plan and a purpose for his life. I told him that whether he accepts my offer or not, that I would not report it to the police. I told him that I've been where he is, but God delivered me from that life and gave me a new one, and He desires the same for him.

By the end of the conversation, I ended up giving him my information and he gave me back my money. I insisted that he keep the money, and by the end of the dream, he became a worthy advocate in the ministry along beside me.

Last Letter to Family Before Coming Home

It was not coincidental that the attempted robbery took place in my neighborhood, that the crime was a robbery involving a gun, that the robber was just a kid, and lastly that I was used to help him. God is looking to acclimate many of you who are reading this book as we speak. Will you lay your all on the altar and answer the call? If so, you need further instructions. Please contact me through the information in the back of this book.

I'd also like to exhort the churches that are in our neighborhoods throughout the Untied States, and ask for your assistance in this dire cause. I believe that it's now time to come out from behind the pulpit and get up off your soft-cushioned pews and stop *having* church and start *being* the Church. It's time to unify, organize, mobilize, strategize, and take back our children out of the hands of the enemy.

It's time for the Church to start walking in the power that was given to them by the Father for the purpose of successfully engaging in combat with the enemy, and coming out on victory's side by taking back all that he stole from us, including our children.

Our children don't need preaching to; they need to know that they're loved, that they're needed, and that they're significant. They need to be made aware of Satan's plan to destroy them, and lastly they need to be told in laymen's terms of God's purpose for their lives, and His plans to prosper them. We have to be hands-on in our efforts of leading them into a better life.

Jesus said that the harvest is great but the laborers are few. The harvest is not in the church buildings; laborers are. The harvest is in those streets throughout our neighborhoods where Satan is having a buffet of a time getting full from the blood of our children.

It's time we gave them a descriptive choice to counter Satan's buy-now-and-pay-later-with-your-life plan, written in small print, then let them decide.

Affirmation of Oneness

Therefore shall a man leave his father and his mother, and shall cleave unto his wife: and they shall be one flesh. I understand the spiritual implications and just how prosperous a marriage would be if a man and a woman were to walk in the fullness of this oneness that God is speaking of. But there's a physical oneness that is demonstrated through sexual intercourse that pictures the very expression of oneness in the Spirit that God is referring to. It has been neglected, misused, and misunderstood throughout the ages.

The spirituality as well as the level of God-given pleasure that personifies this God-given gift has been diminished through the craftiness of the enemy, along with the sinful nature of man. But if we who profess to be spiritual would embrace the reality of this physical connection, that it binds two people together by the exchange or joining of body parts and that it depicts and expresses the very oneness of who we are in relation to one another and how God sees us, I believe that that knowledge would restore the sanctity, desire, joy, pleasure, and regularity of sexual intimacy, with the understanding that this is the will of God for your life.

To neglect it or fail to see it as God sees it can create a doorway for the enemy to use his brush to paint you a picture of how he wants you to see it. Then before you know it, you'll have the world's view of it, and it becomes a chore, one-sided instead of oneness, occasional instead of consistent, and your desire turns into whether or not he or she deserves it, knowing that neither of you have the right to withhold what belongs to the other.

But to keep a balance on the topic, your spiritual oneness needs to be in operation according to the will of God as well; which means that love for one another will be manifested and demonstrated in every area of your lives, always considering the other before or as you do yourself. You are one body; if you stump your toe, there's not a part on your body that says, "I'm OK."

Always pay close attention and know the state and condition of your body. Be careful to respond to any early symptoms of irregularity, knowing if not attended to, could affect the flow of harmony.

Always communicate, and listen intently with an attitude to want to please the other in all things. Sports, hobbies, family, and the ministry come second to him or her, and he or she is second only to God.

With you giving of yourself unconditionally to the other, it's a warranted sacrifice that satisfies the law of God, and keeps the expression of oneness in and out of the bedroom.

Beware of Idols

For some time now, my darling friend and sister in the Lord, Rosie, has been running into a spiritual wall that has all but restricted her from having a productive prayer life, as well as being able to read and understand what God is saying in His Word. However, she has a very productive relationship with her pastor, in whom she can't stop speaking of and giving honor to for doing such an awesome job in ministering and caring for the spiritual needs of God's people.

Although she has been going through financial difficulties for quite some time now, it is disappointing to her that she's unable to give more to his ministry than she has been. But this is a woman who loves the Lord, her pastor, and God's people. There are times when her refrigerator is bare, but it does not create a sense of sluggishness or inconsistency in the time that she willingly and lovingly dedicates to ministering to God's people.

Being that she's been without transportation for months now, lives home alone, and can't reach her appointed destinations, I believe that I'm right in respectfully saying that it's time for the pastor to give. The church was not only instituted and designed to provide spiritual necessities, but the natural necessities of life as well; especially when it pertains to a long-time proven faithful and supportive servant of the congregation.

I do believe that this pastor is all that Rosie says he is in God, and that he means well; but I also believe that he is missing God in procrastinating or failing to aid and assist in catering to the needs of my friend.

My second concern is that Rosie has exalted her pastor above measure and has allowed her relationship to him to stand as a substitution for what's lacking in her relationship with the Father, particularly her prayer life and the reading of God's Word; and my prayer is that he hasn't become an idol unto her.

I know that that is a very dangerous and dry place to be in; one that will disrupt and hinder the flow of God's blessings from being poured freely into your life. It can cloud your vision and prevent you from hearing and seeing God's plans and purposes for your life, and keep you from receiving the very best that God has for you.

For instance, a husband, because the pastor's influence in your life may supersede your husband's, which would cause problems within the home; finances, because your giving to his ministry could be out of control and not Spirit-led, but instead being distributed according to the status in which he holds in your life, as well as his ability and gift to uplift one's spirit when they're down. Although priceless, that does not negate the reality that God is seeking out good stewards that aren't emotional givers but Spirit-led seed sowers.

Most importantly, we know that our God is a jealous God. What man in their right mind desires to give gifts to his wife after finding out that she's cheating or being unfaithful to him? Likewise, when we knowingly or unknowingly give another God's glory or have left the place of giving honor where honor is due, and have moved into the realm of worshipping that person or thing, we are counted as an adulterer in the eyes of the Lord, and nothing good can come from that.

Unforgiveness

If you ever want to deny the enemy of one of his most productive weapons in his arsenal, try forgiving those who have wronged you. There's nothing more powerful and liberating than that. That is one stronghold that will blur your vision and restrict you from seeing and experiencing the manifested blessings that God has already shown you and ordained for you to have.

The reason why Satan is so successful in this area of our lives, especially those who are incarcerated, is simply because those who we feel have wronged us aren't talked about or seen for years due to our lengthy stay in prison. So while you're wondering why your blessings are being held up, God is saying it's because you haven't acknowledged or forsaken this unforgiveness that has been embedded in your heart.

God knows that if not dealt with while in prison, that our reaction towards them when we see them after getting out could not only rob Him of His glory, but land us back in prison as well.

So wisdom urges us to take an inventory of our lives in relation to our attitude towards everyone who may have wronged us in one

Last Letter to Family Before Coming Home

way or the other, unless prolonging your stay in prison is really not all that important.

One way of resolving this issue is to diligently search your heart and revisit every past relationship to determine whether or not it ended in a negative way. And yes, that includes those who may have made statements against you or testified against you in trial.

Once you've individually surveyed each person and tested the condition of your heart towards them by simply praying for their well-being and asking God to bless them, if there's a free flow in your spirit and you truly desire to see them blessed, then you are liberated from the guilt and repercussions that come with unforgiveness.

On the other hand, if you've discovered that you do have an issue with someone from the past, then I urge you to continue to proclaim these blessings in their lives until it takes root in your spirit, as well as asking God for help in this area of your life, until having their best interest at heart becomes a living reality. Receiving all that God has for you depends on it.

In Response to Last Letter Before Coming Home

As of late, I haven't received many responses regarding the recent letter to my family. Some have chosen to be silent on the matter. Hopefully that's a sign of regret which brings about a change; while one aunt in particular took offense to it, and vehemently refused to be identified with any parts of the letter. An old friend once told me that a hit dog will holler.

Although there's much evidence from the past to refute her argument, wisdom led me to pursue peace, and allow her the liberty to hold on to her state of denial. Besides, my reason for writing the letter had nothing to do with wanting a continued dialogue or debate concerning issues that they're unwilling to deal with.

My only endeavor was to state the obvious, which was to show them that they were their worst enemy; and to establish an understanding between them and myself regarding my purpose and every intention to let nothing or no one stand in the way of fulfilling it.

Lastly, to let them know that there will always be an open door to anyone who wants my help in becoming and having all that God desires for them. Admittedly, it's a hurtful feeling seeing my loved ones go through life without God's divine presence sustaining them; and the hurt intensifies when I consider whether or not some will respond to or reject the Lord's plan for their lives. Although those feelings always seem to dissipate when I consider just how awesome my God is and the fact that He saved me. That is when I realize there's much hope for my family.

13
When Faith Fails, Trust

It's never easy sustaining one's faith over the course of many years while expecting the Lord to do the miraculous in your situation, especially when every possible avenue that the eye can see has reached a dead end.

What do you do when faced with this dilemma, after being fully persuaded that God said He would deliver, but because of the many doors that have slammed in your face, it seems as though you've been waiting on your breakthrough for so long until your faith begins to falter along the way? You simply trust Him.

When we add trust to our foundation, we're telling God that we're going to see it to the very end; that even though we may get knocked off our high horse more than a few times, and we're too weak to travel, we're going to lean on You, Lord, and trust You to carry us the rest of the way.

I would be dishonest with you if I were to tell you that my faith didn't waiver at times along this journey. But even in my darkest of hours, God's words of deliverance, which He had spoken to me in the beginning, were all that a struggling Christian was able to cling to. When all else had failed, losing my trial, my appeals, lawyers had taken all of my money, the Department of Justice wasn't willing to expose their own under that administration for the sake of justice, no civil rights organizations would stand with me. So there were no other legal avenues available for me to pursue.

But I had a word from the Lord that never ceased from speaking. Therefore, I never ceased from responding on this wise, Father, even though it looks like all hope is lost and I'm never getting out of prison. Even though I feel spiritually drained, You said that You would deliver me. You said that You would confound and expose the government. You said that I would come out with much more than I had coming in, and that You would use me in a mighty way that You might be glorified.

So Father, I trust You in spite of the tears, the fears, and the multitude of years wherein I expected to see the salvation of the Lord manifest in my situation.

Trust is the backbone to your faith. When nothing else seems to be working, trust God.

I Don't Want to Miss God in This

I attended church service on the other night, and the preacher talked about the process of knowing how to hear from God, and how we shouldn't get discouraged when we miss Him. He shared one of his past experiences when he was in a season of fasting and praying, and God revealed to him that he would be delivered from his present condition within five years. Being fully persuaded that it was of God, he went before the church to share the good news that he believed God had given him.

After the five years had passed and it was obvious that he had missed God, he became upset with the Lord and asked Him how He could have deceived him, and allowed him to proclaim a lie to His people.

The preacher went on to say that the Lord later revealed to him that when he sought an answer from Him concerning his situation, there was already a preconceived notion in his heart of what he had expected God's response to be.

God told him that wasn't His voice that he had heard, and that, "The enemy gave you what you wanted to hear in an attempt to discredit you and to silence you before My people. Even though My signature that you heard from Me is peace, you were walking in a false sense of peace. It is true that you did hear a word, but because it had confirmed what was already in your heart, you ran with it without considering where it came from."

God went on to say that, "Missing Me comes with the process of getting more familiar with and knowing My voice. I don't get angry with you when you miss Me; but I do expect for you to come clean with everyone that you may have unintentionally deceived, that they may be aware and educated, and hopefully deterred from making the same mistakes."

Now that was a Word that really helped me to walk more cautiously before saying, "God said." It also had me thinking whether or not I might have missed God in believing that He was behind all of the influences that led me to believe that He wants me to marry Rosie.

God knows that I love her with the *agape* kind of love and want the very best for her, even if that means taking her hand in marriage. But so does Satan, and he would want nothing more than to manipulate me into a marriage that wasn't influenced or ordained by God.

Yes, Rosie is an amazing woman of God, and yes, I do want to be a blessing to her, and will, but I refuse to miss God concerning this life-lasting union. That's not to say it's not the Lord's will for us to get married, but realizing that it's not, too late, could possibly cause one to live a life in bondage. To later realize that I missed God, and that Satan used my love for God and Rosie against me, could create a suppressed sense of resentment.

That's not God's will for us. He desires for us to walk in liberty, and to live in truth, and willfully make decisions according to that truth. Therefore, God's wisdom provokes me to apologize to my readers for possibly missing God in this matter, and to bear with me until after we've spent some quality time together after I've been released, OK?

Rosie's Birthday

Today is April 4, 2011, a day after Rosie's birthday and three days before mine. I was hoping that God would allow us to spend our birthday together on the outside, although as of yet, it's not a lost cause. Still, I'm encouraged and excited in knowing that the day is at hand where we'll be able to celebrate past and future occasions together.

After calling her to wish her a happy birthday, it was a little disturbing to know that she and a very close sister and friend in the Lord had to collectively and scarcely come up with enough money to go out to dinner for her birthday.

You would think that people would be lined up to honor this kindhearted, selfless, and anointed woman of God, who as you know, has dedicated her life to serving. But the truth of the matter is, there were some who are close to her who neglected to sacrifice as much as two minutes of their time to call her and to wish her a happy birthday.

Proverbs 3:27 teaches us to withhold no good thing from them to whom it is due, when it is in the power of thine hand to do it. That is why I'm convinced that there is no power in religion and religious mindsets. It does not produce love; neither does it perfect character in a person, which enables you to demonstrate the fruits of the Spirit in our everyday lives.

All religion does is gives us a mask to hide behind. We put it on just before leaving home on our way to church and take it off while leaving the church premises. We go to church wearing the finest of outfits, hoping that our attire will hide the condition of our heart; shaking hands, hugging, giving fixed smiles while greeting those whom we may have talked about all throughout the week in an unfavorable manner.

God has allowed a twofold occurrence to take place in the lives of His people that is beneficial to us all, given the proper response. Any time we as Christians experience the trials and tribulations of life which come to test us, if we take the right approach while going through them, such as praising and thanking God in spite of how things may look, and knowing that you're going to come out on victory's side simply because you know that no weapon formed against you shall prosper, and that you're more than a conqueror, not only do you strip it of its power and effect over your life, but once you've prevailed, it produces a greater level of strength, patience, maturity, faith, and dependence on our God, just to name a few.

The second thing that it does is that while you're going through your test, it affords an opportunity for your brothers and sisters in the Kingdom who are a little more fortunate than you are to minister to your necessities. It puts a balance on Paul's message to the Philippians when he told them that he knew how to be abased and how to abound; to be full and how to be hungry. Even though this was at a time when the Philippians were ministering to his needs, he was stating the obvious, which was the fact that he had been through many occasions when he could have used a little help; and those occasions matured and perfected him in the field of going through.

One identifiable trait found in a child of God that has gone through is perseverance. On the other hand, one of the identifiable marks found in a child of God who has witnessed someone going through is their desire to provide or care for them according to one's need.

We don't want to be found standing before the Lord hearing Him recite that famous speech, "Depart from Me, for I was hungry and you fed Me not; thirsty and you gave Me no drink; a stranger and you took Me not in; naked, and ye clothed Me not; sick, and in prison, and ye visited me not; for inasmuch as ye have did it not to one of the least of these, ye did it not to Me."

My Birthday

April the 8th, a day after my birthday. I thought I'd wait until after it had passed so that I could give you a brief description on how it went.

Unlike Rosie's birthday, I received several gifts from brothers in the Lord that are in prison with me, along with some who vowed to present me with one the following week. You might ask, what kind of gift can you get or give in prison? Well, some go to the commissary and buy an ice cream and/or a box of cakes; while others may combine various items and fix you a little microwave dinner. Now this may not seem like much to those who are on the outside, but for us, it's the equivalent to a steak or seafood dinner.

It's not a small thing for those in prison to give out of their limited resources. It's not like we make minimum wage or receive a substantial salary from home every month. The best job on the compound only pays forty-five cents an hour max; and you would be doing good if you received fifty dollars a month from home. But that's the thing about the *agape* kind of love; it's not limited or dependent upon your condition or situation. It compels you to graciously give to those to whom it is due, when it is in thine power to do it.

I also received some birthday money from my mother, along with a card from Rosie, one of my daughters, and three from her mother, with instructions not to open one of them until the seventeenth. I don't know what that's about, but in reading the other two cards from her, I can tell that she's about to start campaigning for the position of becoming Mrs. Malone.

One thing that is a certainty with women from past relationships, once they hear any news concerning you being released from prison, their motives to rekindle old flames become apparent. I feel as though it's rather selfish of them as well as arrogant to think that they should be given the privilege of picking up where the relationship left off after years of emotional, mental, financial, and even spiritual neglect for those who profess to be Christians.

Now don't get me wrong; I believe in second chances. But there's one thing that adversity reveals in a person: their heart. Sometimes it's not necessarily what you do, but how and why in which you do it, although we know that there are certain situations where the person that's being locked up has messed up in such a way that it leaves a person with nothing that's worth fighting for. However, with this particular woman, we were once engaged, and she was supposed to have been the one.

She has a good heart; she's just not conditioned for a long-distance prison relationship, in which I've come to understand at this point in my life, no one should have to be bound to such an abnormal life except it be voluntary. So although she's a lovely person with history, there's no future for us due to two simple *truths*.

Even though she is one who was raised in the church, she's yet to surrender her life to the Lord. The second thing is, there's Rosie. No one will be considered without knowing whether or not it is truly the Lord's will for us to cut the cake. And if it's not, she has set the bar so high, now that I've witnessed what an anointed, committed, and totally surrendered woman of God looks like, I couldn't settle for just an average Christian woman who professes to be saved, but lacks the power.

I am thankful that we are good friends still, and I'm confident that my convictions regarding the principles in which I now live by won't change that.

A Family Reunion

Well, as always, without notice, my sleep was interrupted at 4:00 a.m. in the morning by a correction officer instructing me to get ready for suicide watch. Upon my arrival and after some time had passed, I began to reflect on the recent news that the Malone family is about to have our first family reunion in June, which is only about two months away. Apparently someone who is on my grandfather's side is sponsoring the event.

Considering all that has gone on over the years, and the various issues that have literally destroyed the structure of my immediate family, I perceive this to be a timely blessing and an answered prayer that could help reconcile and restore the family values that we once upheld and demonstrated towards one another.

The only thing that I see is lacking and could attribute to making this a successful and monumental milestone would be my attendance. But God is so awesome, and there's nothing that I would put past Him. If He wants me there, I'll be there. So there's no need to be wrestling and struggling with that.

Accompanied with this exciting news, some other news had surfaced that didn't seem quite as exciting to some. My family had received an unexpected visit from a twenty-two-year-old young lady who claims to be my recently deceased ninety-four-year-old grandfather's daughter.

To prevent you from stopping to tally up the years in order to calculate how old my grandfather was when he supposedly had impregnated the young lady's mother, I've done it for you; he would have been seventy-one years old at the time.

And for those of you who are curious to know how old the child's mother was at the time, from my understanding she was in her mid-twenties. I also understand that there's supposed to be certain documents on file that could confirm the validity of her allegation. But we all know that my grandfather had a history and a reputation of being seen with younger women, to say the least.

I can recall a certain time in my life when I was living in my dark days, that I had actually interviewed, or rather, questioned a young lady that we believed was having relations with him. I remember paying her a substantial amount of money just to tell me the truth regarding my granddaddy's ability to function in a sexual manner. I know that it was a rather odd question, but I got tired of wondering what was really going on with him.

Understanding that this information would stay between the two of us, and that it was contingent upon the truth, she immediately gave my granddaddy *two thumbs up*, emphasis added. So I'm not blown away or that surprised by the news. If it's true, I just pray that the family will embrace her and treat her a little better than they've treated one another.

Remembering Daddy on His Birthday

Today is April the 18th, a day after Daddy's birthday. His birthday being ten days after mine reminded me of the many things that we had in common. Of course, when I say "Daddy," I'm referring to my granddaddy.

Since the day I was born and was able to pronounce words, I've always called him "Daddy" because that's what he has always been to me. But I just want to acknowledge him on today as I'm sure I will do on April the 17th for many years to come, if the Lord says the same.

I did call home to see how the family was doing. It was nice to hear that some in the family had come together to celebrate and to honor him on this memorable occasion. I believe that Daddy's life will always be remembered, celebrated, and bring much laughter, as well as many tears.

As I reflect back on his life, one of several moments flashed through my mind: remembering my faults, and the first time that I stood before a judge to be sentenced to prison. The judge asked if there was anyone who would like to speak on my behalf. My daddy stood up and began to give a brief description of how he had raised me from a baby, while using his hands to illustrate just how small I was at that time.

Although I appreciated and loved him for speaking on my behalf, the tears that flooded down my face as a result of how moved I was over his words brought about a sense of embarrassment, being that

I was now a part of a system and an environment that says you have to at least appear to be mentally tough, and that tears have no place here. Well, at least not in the open. So my prayer was that this part of the process would soon come to an end so that I could regroup and regain my composure before I was to be escorted back to the holding cell, where I would be surrounded by other prisoners.

Daddy has always been there for me when I needed him. Of course there were times when he had done some things that didn't make much sense to me, but the mere thought of those moments creates lots of laughs. Like the times when I would be lying in the bed early in the morning with my wife at the time, usually just having a conversation with the door shut. Suddenly out of nowhere Daddy would come over unannounced and rush into our bedroom like he was the police, scaring the mess out of the both of us! Although his reason for coming over so early was to see if I had any money, I couldn't help but wonder whether or not Daddy was trying to sneak a peak at a little early morning entertainment! That probably wasn't the case, but I just never understood why he never knocked before coming in.

Well, thank you for a lifetime of memories, Daddy, You'll never be forgotten. Happy birthday.

14
Should Christians Have the Liberty to Engage in Explicit Sexual Practices with Their Spouse, Such as Oral Sex?

What has been a frequently discussed topic among Christians lately is whether or not oral sex is permissible in the bedroom between married couples in the eyes of God. Many church leaders today have concluded that just about anything goes between a husband and his wife within the confines of their bedroom and that it is honorable in the sight of God, and they've passed this same information on to their parishioners.

The main Scripture in which they cling to in order to promote this ungodly and perverted practice is found in the book of Hebrews, chapter 13 verse 4, which states that marriage is honorable in all, and the bed undefiled; but whoremongers and adulterers God will judge.

I can see how it's possible for some to misinterpret this Scripture, especially for Christians who have experienced this sexual practice for quite some time and have enjoyed it, and are looking for a remotely and seemingly unclear Scripture that will support their undisciplined sexual appetite.

Now don't misunderstand me; I'm not bashing or condemning my beloved brothers and sisters in Christ, and I'm not trying to make a new doctrine out of this. But I sincerely believe that the truth of the matter is not only found in Scripture, but it also lies within your conscience, as well as in nature. If that be the case, I'd like to think that every believer would want to know it, that we might choose to exercise control over the flesh in order to please and obey the One who has called us to holiness.

Now as we take a closer look at this Scripture, we find that God is simply making a distinction between the bed or sexual intercourse of a married couple, as opposed to whoremongers and adulterers. It is not referring to how you do what you do in your bedroom, but rather giving you the right to do it while simultaneously forbidding all others from practicing it.

There are multiple words that are found in the New Testament that are not just limited to condemning the practice of homosexuality, but all manner of sexual perversion, which means to stray away from the right or normal way of God's intended purpose, as well as sexual indulgence, and failing to restrain from one's sexual appetite; words such as inordinate, incontinence, uncleanness, lasciviousness, wantonness, and sexual perversion, etc.

You might say that if God didn't want us to do that, then He would have plainly stated it in His Word. Well, God didn't plainly say that gambling is forbidden, but we as Christians have come to understand that gambling is a sin. Besides, there's no evidence to my knowledge that this was a common practice until long after the Bible was written. But I think it was wise of God to put a broad range of perverted sexual terms in the Bible that would cover everything that was and was to come from the perverted imagination of man.

Many of us can remember years ago when this thing called oral sex had first hit the scene. And even if you were persuaded to try it, you would be too ashamed and embarrassed to openly discuss it with others. Why? Because your conscience confirmed that it wasn't a normal or natural thing to do.

Not only that, but we've all witnessed that it is a common and a natural thing for a dog to do to another dog, which stands to reason that maybe it's not for a child of God, or human being, for that matter, who is made in the likeness and image of God. But because of years of indulging, we've become so desensitized and our conscience has become seared until talking about it has become almost as easy as conversing about our favorite foods.

I was reading an article in the March 2012 issue of *Men's Journal* which gives even more credence as to why oral sex should be avoided. Not only is oral sex unnatural, there is research to indicate that it can also lead to throat cancer. The human papillomavirus, or HPV, is the most common sexually transmitted disease in the United States. Researchers see a connection between the increasing popularity of oral sex and a rise in the number of cases of throat cancer, which has increased 225 percent in the last sixteen years, affecting men more than women. While most people who contract HPV get rid of the virus in a few years and the number of men who contract it is still very small, researchers believe there is nothing a heterosexual man with a normal sex life can do to protect himself from contracting it. There is also no way to detect it until the infected person becomes sick, at which time it is often too late to treat as the cancer may have spread to the lymph nodes. According to the article, "40 percent of the 36,000 people diagnosed each year with oral cancer will die from the disease within five years," and "oral cancer ranked as the seventh most common cancer among men in the U.S between 1992 and 2001, the most recent data available." There are vaccines that can be given to young boys and girls, but they are costly for the required three shots, and controversial as well, since they are given to prevent cancer from sexual activity, and many parents aren't willing to expose their young children to them. (Gardiner Harris, "Can Oral Sex Cause Cancer?" *Men's Journal*, March 2012, 59-60).

So the problem is this. Many of us as Christians have catered to the flesh for so long in this area while we were in the world, until oral sex has become the beginning of the process for a normal sexual encounter with our spouse. And because the results are rewarding to the flesh, the power behind its influence won't allow many of us to depart from it—not even for Jesus Himself.

Satan has deceived us with a mandate that we have to do this in order to be pleased and to please our significant other. You know how it goes. If you don't, then someone else will. This is the world's way of thinking, just as it was the world in which we were introduced to this perverted way of sexual intercourse. And it has no place in the life of God's people.

When God had first given us the gift of sexual intercourse long before there was oral sex, it produced pleasure, and it will continue to without it. God is not saying we must be robots in the bedroom. We as men need to be leaders, even in our bedroom, embracing the art of foreplay and learning the craft of romance.

We need to be reminded that sex is a gift, and with receiving a gift comes anticipation, careful handling, like a treasure to behold.

And once we've unwrapped our gift, we should take our time admiring it with offerings of scented candles, soft music, a modest toast of wine before the celebration, then after patience has had her perfect work, gently enjoy the oneness with your very own.

It is important to understand that this seed of perversion is deeply embedded in some of our sisters as well as brothers within the church. This is why we must be prudent in selecting a mate, being fully persuaded that he or she is of the same like mind.

This is not an issue that we address after proposing, not to mention marriage. It wouldn't be wise to marry without knowing the expectations of the one that you could potentially spend the rest of your life with. The last thing that you would want to do is put the one you love in bondage.

We can't expect to have two different understandings and convictions regarding something so prevalent in the bedroom in the hearts of many. That alone could put you on a path that is destined for disaster.

It is my heart's desire that every believer will search this matter out and take it before the Lord without any preconceived resolution, with an endeavor to know the mind of God, and to please Him in this matter, and not ourselves.

My Babies Are Having Babies

One of the most important things at this point in my life is the reverence that my daughters have for their father. It's not something that I take for granted; neither do I take credit for such a profound gift; for I know that it is the Lord who has graced me with His character and ability to be a productive father while in prison. Not only that, but I've come to a rare conclusion that unlike most in my situation, my daughters are fully persuaded that their father is a man of God. To God be the glory!

In building our relationship on these terms, with distance being the obstacle, I took the approach of laying a foundation based on transparency. One of the principles in which we were to try and establish was that even though I was their father as well as a Christian, there was nothing that we couldn't discuss or share with one another. And although they try hard not to do anything that they feel would disappoint me, I try to teach them to take comfort in the fact that mistakes are a part of life. What matters is how you deal with them. My only standard is that we deal with them together.

It is true that all of my daughters are adults; the youngest is going on twenty-one years old and the oldest will be twenty-three this year. And although I try to instill responsibility along with maturity in them, I believe that even when they reach the age of fifty, they will still be Daddy's little girls.

Anyway, everything has been great between us, and they often bring tears to my eyes by telling me that I'm the best daddy in the world. So I'm thankful for the relationship that we have, and I'm looking forward to it getting even better as we continue to embrace the liberty and simplicity that help stabilize our foundation.

Having said that, no one really knows just how much pressure a foundation can stand and whether or not it needs to be strengthened unless it is tested and tried by a storm with a sufficient amount of force. Well, our storm came last month, with not one, but two twisters. And although it did some damage, all was not lost. We not only survived it; we were also able to do some repairs and become better prepared for future catastrophes.

When I found out in the same month that two of my daughters were pregnant, I must admit it was a bit challenging. But the way in which it was discovered contradicted the basis of our foundation. And that consequently gave power to the nature of the storm.

We mustn't allow the pressure that problems tend to produce cloud our perspective on what's most important. Failing to do so usually causes a person to see something that is not really there, and that adds to or even creates another problem.

Now when it comes to my girls, clearly the most important thing is our relationship and the bond that we have established, which was built on trust. But the fear of not knowing how I would respond and not wanting to disappoint me caused one to conceal the matter for several months, while continuously confiding in someone close to me for answers or counseling on how to tell me, which was something I didn't find out until after the fact. But thankfully her mother and I are close.

So being that she told me in secret, I had to go through a season of several phone conversations with my daughter, while being aware of the struggle that she was having to bear of needing to tell me something that I already knew; something that was difficult for me to do. But it finally came to an end once her mother relieved her of the responsibility by letting her know that she had already told me the news, which brought about a heightened sense of nervousness as well as relief for her.

On the other hand, my other daughter took a different approach. Although she may have succeeded in sharing the news with me in a timely manner, the pressure of anticipating my response caused her to panic, and it seemed as though the reality of who she knew her father to be somehow got lost in the moment. As she was telling me the news, she uncharacteristically asked me not to judge her.

At that time, I had knowledge that two of my three daughters were pregnant, and I had come to realize that the problem was not found in their pregnancy, but rather in their response towards it as it pertained to me.

Sure my daughter told me she didn't know what she was thinking when she had asked me not to judge her, after we had talked about it. And my other daughter agreed not to withhold anything else from me, no matter how hard it may be for her to tell me. But this thing left me wondering whether or not this was all about their respect for me, and their endeavor to make me proud of them; or could I be indirectly putting added pressure on my babies to succeed?

I know that I'm not judgmental towards them, but perhaps I'm sometimes overzealous with my talks of wanting them to live for the Lord. And maybe I've unconsciously presented myself to them as this super Christian who no longer makes mistakes.

It's an awful and unhealthy thing for a father to have become dehumanized in the minds and perceptions of his children. So maybe the imperfection in our foundation lies with me.

As I reflect back to the many heart-to-heart discussions that my children and I had during my post-Christian life, I can't help but wonder whether or not the atmosphere for them was more like one making a confession to a priest as opposed to a daughter running into the comforting arms of a loving and understanding father.

This may or may not be an accurate assumption. Nevertheless, I've vowed to become much more conscious as well as sensitive when it comes to being able to identify with my children in dealing with faults and failures. Not in the sense of giving them a pass to glory in or to relish in it, but rather helping them to see that we all miss the mark, including their daddy. And it is incumbent upon us all to learn from it, and try to get it right the next time, and not to deviate from that pattern until we do.

I once heard a preacher say that winners are made of failures who didn't quit; I concur.

Suicide Watch Again?

It's really becoming disturbing that my sleep is being interrupted so frequently to go and do suicide watch. Not that my sleep is more important than ministering to these men for the purpose of restoring hope back into their lives; but my beefs with the enemy, Satan himself, who appears to be availing in his mission of seeking to steal, kill, and destroy the lives of many. And the rapid increase of suicide watches that I've recently been privy to and have served in is indicative to this reality.

After sitting with and having lengthy conversations with this particular individual, I discovered that his condition and mental state was far more severe than of those I've previously encountered. Not that I'm diminishing the condition or the importance of their lives; it's just that their profile fits one who had succumbed to the pressure of having to do what seemed to be an insurmountable sentence to serve.

On the contrary; the person that I'm currently attending to doesn't have a problem with neither has he ever had a problem with doing time, especially considering the fact that this is about his fifth time coming back to prison. So doing time is like a walk in the park to him. But after spending hours talking with him, and hearing this man's story, my heart went out to him like none other.

Being that I've been given the ministry of reconciliation, along with the power and authority over the enemy, I knew that I had walked into a spiritual battle, and that my mission was clear, which was to engage in spiritual warfare with the enemy in order to set at liberty this man's soul that was obviously under the influence of demonic oppression. To bring you up to speed, allow me to give you a brief description of his history according to his recollection.

Unfortunately, he was raised up around gang violence all of his life, having lived in one of the worst areas in the heart of Chicago. Witnessing death and killings at an early age was the norm for him. But his biggest problem was having seen it in his very own family in such an unforgettable way. I mean, to witness your father blow his brains out, your uncle hang himself, and to start hearing voices at the age of eight years old instructing you to kill even yourself, and to respond by drinking almost a gallon of bleach, which was the first of various attempts, gives you some indication that this young man has undoubtedly lived a very problematic and troublesome life, to say the least.

Not to mention the fact that his little boy has been experiencing a learning disorder in school, and one can only hope that he hasn't been affected by this suicidal spirit that has become evident as well as prevalent within his family, commonly known as a generational curse.

It didn't take long after staring into this person's eyes and hearing his manner of conversation that he not only felt helpless against the power of the enemy, but that he eagerly desired to be liberated from it. Being mindful not to overwhelm him with much religious propaganda, I set out to patiently listen to his every word in order to know and discern the condition of his heart, along with every possible demonic influence that needed to be dealt with. My main purpose was to help him to see that I loved him with a Godly love, and that God loved him more and wanted to set him free.

What angers me the most isn't necessarily the progression of Satan's attack on the lives of the defenseless at the facility, but rather the digression of power in the lives of the believer. The people of God here have denied the power that has been freely given to them by the omnipotent God as a result of their pursuit of fulfilling their desire to be great in the Kingdom. Winning souls has become so meager, and beneath their seemingly self-given callings and titles, that some have become so reckless in their endeavor to promote themselves until it's not only setting an erroneous and bad pattern for the young believers to follow, but it has also become a distraction as well as a hindrance for potential candidates for salvation.

It seems as though I've been down this road with you before concerning this matter; but for the moment, the enemy continues to exploit this particular weakness within the body. So while I've consulted with the Lord on this matter and have obeyed His instructions, please allow me to do a little venting every now and then until the Lord works this thing out.

Anyway, where was I? Oh yeah. After he became persuaded of my intentions and motives towards him, that they were only good, he trusted me to pray with him and to usurp my God-given authority over the enemy, demanding that he vacate the premises.

While speaking on this subject, I'm reminded of the many books and mindsets today in the Christian world that have attempted to give instructions on the spiritual application of this contentious duty that we've been given. Some have explained away the simplicity of the requirements, as well as the procedural steps towards prevailing in this matter. It has become so philosophical and sophisticated that many believers not only fear engaging in spiritual warfare, but they've come to feel inadequate.

Many leaders in Christendom fail to properly educate and prepare their parishioners for this kind of task at the expense of maintaining their superiority and status of supernatural appearance. I believe that the Bible is clear in its teachings on how to successfully dethrone, cast out, and the departing of any demonic influences in a person's life. And I believe that a careful study on these following Scriptures will bear out this truth.

Any believer that has believed on and trusted in the Name of Jesus, has made Him Lord, living an obedient life, along with much prayer and fasting, and understands through faith that the power is in the Name of JESUS, has the legal right to evict and send any demon from hell packing and running. Matthew 10:5-8, Luke 9:1, Mark 9:38-40, John 14:13, Mark 16:16-18, Matthew 17:16-21, Mark 9:17-29, Acts 19:13-15, Matthew 7:21-23. There are other Scriptures that will support this position, but I believe these will do. Back to the matter at hand.

After we had concluded our business, he went fast to sleep. The very next morning after I had arrived, I noticed a change in his countenance, as well as in his conversation, as one that has been set free. I encouraged him to seriously consider giving his life to the Lord to prevent the enemy from ever returning to his old residence. I vowed to continue to intercede in prayer on his behalf, and to be instrumental in his life, endeavoring to see fruit that would lead to repentance.

The very next day the psychiatrist found him fit to return back to the compound. He agreed to attend church with me in a few days. I'll let you know when there's a change in his disposition as it pertains to eternity.

15
It's for Her Good Also That I Be Not Named Amongst Those of a Bad Report

While considering a couple of recent relationship breakups involving men who are about to leave prison and those that have already departed, I was reminded of one of many stigmas that are attached to men who are incarcerated. You know the one; those of us who prey on lonely women for the purposes of finances, visits, and just to help make our bid or time of incarceration as easy as possible, only to dump them once we've been released or begin to see light at the end of the tunnel.

Understanding that to be true, and not wanting to be mistakenly associated in that number, it caused me to reflect back on my relationship with Rosie. God only knows the intents of my heart, that I mean to do her good and not harm all the days of her life. Realizing that this doesn't necessarily include being her husband, the desires and expectations of others, including her own, might beg to differ.

Even though I've made it clear to her, my endeavor to be a blessing to her and that marriage wasn't part of the package unless God says differently, still I'm aware of her aspirations of one day possibly becoming Mrs. Malone. So being that I love her and would do nothing to intentionally hurt my dear friend, the potential of doing so is there. What do I do?

I've fought against my personality and preference for so long, like it was a crime or sin to even have one, as though God had nothing to do with me being this way. During the process of this struggle I endured a brief season of endlessly having uncontrollable thoughts and dreams of this fifty-five-year-old woman of God, and for a time, I contributed it to God's doing. In my ignorance, I guess I assumed that He was miraculously changing my makeup or redirecting my desire from the physical to the spiritual aspect of a woman.

Although where a woman is spiritual is most important, I believe that we would be dehumanizing ourselves as well as putting oneself in bondage if we attempt to suppress or consider who or what we're attracted to. I'm persuaded that this is why the Lord forbade me to tell Rosie my misguided decision to marry her, not knowing that it wasn't from Him.

Being in the vulnerable state of living in prison for many years and consistently communing with the opposite sex has the potential of causing one to settle for someone that you're not compatible with. Even though that person is lovely and possesses their own special qualities, they don't identify with the real you. But because you're emotionally sensitive and have been placed in an abnormal environment, you tend to settle and to see something that's not really there or real.

So I'll tell you what I did; I did that which was difficult and wrote her a letter reiterating the parameters that define the nature of our relationship. Even though I wrote it with the softest tone and choicest of words I could find, after talking with her in regards to the letter, I realized my efforts to minimize the disappointment was hopeless. Her rebuttal was that I postpone this unwelcomed affirmation until after I'm released to see whether or not the Lord says the same.

As hard as it was for me not to give in to her request for the sake of wanting her to feel better, I knew that her pain as well as mine would be much worse if I were to wait and make my decision once I'm out, providing that it wouldn't be a favorable one. If it be God's will to unite us together as husband and wife on the outside, surely He could do it in spite of our plans or expectations to do otherwise.

So unfortunately, it grieved me to maintain my position, and to endure listening to the regretful sound of her voice. But I'm persuaded that once this chapter of my life has ended as it pertains to my incarceration, she'll find closure in the fact that I'll always be there for her as her friend and beloved brother in the Lord—ALWAYS.

That Which I Had Failed to Do

Well, it's been over a week now since I last talked with Rosie, which is longer than normal. But the frequent conversations, I believe, have been the main reason behind the emotional attachments that we've recently had to address. To continue that same pattern would be rather foolish, to say the least. Although I miss the more frequent conversations with her, the risk of adding more fuel to the fire warrants the sacrifice.

While dialing her number, expecting a conversation of carefully chosen words, I was reluctantly greeted with a bit of bad news. After an effort of trying to prepare me before giving me the news, she finally told me that my son was arrested for drugs, along with an automatic weapon.

All at once, I immediately felt his pain, accompanied with the pain of a father who felt he had let his son down by leaving a bad example for him to follow, and failing to return in time in order to right the wrong, that his son might have a fighting chance of not following in his father's footsteps.

It has been a constant prayer of mine that the Lord would allow me the opportunity to make it out of prison in order to help save my son's life. But that was the vehicle in which the Lord had used to save mine. Perhaps He chose the same for my son. Although we usually prefer Him to do things our way, His way is always best.

Maybe He saw death coming and chose prison instead in order to hide him for a season as a token of honoring His servant's request to preserve the life of his seed. But in spite of the circumstance and how drastic it may seem or how I might feel, my trust is in the King of Glory.

Still I can't help but acknowledge the picture that is presented; one that is shown on a daily basis: fathers being locked away for a long time unjustly for a nonviolent crime, only for their children to be raised and fathered by a neighborhood of fatherless peers who can only give you what they've been given—a false sense of love, along with the same plan of survival that they were told their father once used before going to prison.

It's an ugly picture, and at the risk of sounding pessimistic, it is one that resembles a highly calculated plan—one that would psychologically enslave a particular group of people and subtly lure them to prison for generations to come.

How do you remedy such a horrific catastrophe? Well, you would think getting them to see and admit their error would bring about some sort of resolve. But then again, if this seemingly foolproof strategy didn't bring out retribution from slavery, why would a different form of slavery bring about a favorable resolution?

Please understand that when I use the words "their" or "them," I'm referring to any and all of those who participated or took part in creating, building, and supporting a system that would even have the potential to destroy a life without merit, let alone a significant portion of an entire race of people. Back to the matter at hand.

In admitting their mistakes concerning the inhumane sentences that were given to thousands upon thousands of black men who are currently in prison, they responded on this wise and I'm paraphrasing: We know and admit that we've made a mistake. However, we've given entirely too many men illegal sentences, and we can't correct the problem because it would open up the floodgates and allow too many criminals back on the streets with nothing more to do but commit more crimes.

Wow! What an excuse. How about: Because of our error in creating laws that targeted and discriminated against a particular group of people which resulted in them serving a significant number of years beyond what the law required, which ultimately destroyed families, we're going to do the right thing and release them. And even though we can't put a price on their life, we're going to compensate them with enough money to get them settled and to live off of according to the number of years that were taken from them, as well as for their inconvenience.

That is so gangster and criminal in nature, to admit to breaking or violating the law, and in the same breath, boldly proclaim your endeavor to stay the course. We are a nation who desperately needs to repent and reconcile with those that we've offended while there's still time.

I believe that God has and is demonstrating His disappointment as well as His lack of patience with us as of late by allowing a rapid increase in killer storms that have claimed the lives of many, as well as this financial burden that this nation has had to endure over the past four to five years.

As a whole, we are in error concerning a number of things that have already been highlighted and addressed by many. Therefore, I don't see the need to continue to beat a dead horse, but rather to assist in sounding the alarm by simply proclaiming the need for an inward change, that God's anger might be appeased; that His grace may be extended.

An Emotional Father's Day

Well, several days have passed since Father's Day, and for men who are in prison, as well as their children, it tends to be emotional. Particularly this year's Father's Day here at FCI Jesup.

To start the day off, there's an early morning Sunday church service, and I'm scheduled to lead a song before a large congregation, something that has always been challenging for me. Being nervous is just something I can never get used to, even though after about the first thirty seconds into it, whether I'm singing or ministering, the Holy Spirit always takes over and settles me and uses me in an awesome way.

Rightfully so, I'm always careful to address my issue and assure Him that I'm totally dependent upon His power and anointing in order to fulfill His purpose, which is to exhort and to edify the people of God. So while I'm minutes away from the moment at hand, I was asked by the chaplain to pray for the servant leaders. *Really, God!* I thought to myself; *I'm to preach the sermon too.*

One thing that I've come to learn about the Father of us all, when you admit your weaknesses and rely solely on His strength and power, He always shows up in a mighty way. For the Bible tells us that His strength is made perfect in weakness.

Anyway, the prayer was so inspiring, and I was told by more than a few just how amazing the delivery of that song was. I silently

It's for Her Good Also That I Be Not Named Amongst Those of a Bad Report

agreed. It was as though God had said, "You can sit down now, my son. I'll take it from here." And boy, did He! Wow! Thanks, Dad!

As the choir sat down, expecting to hear a powerful Father's Day sermon by the chaplain, he got up and said that he wanted to do something different for this occasion. He said that he was going to sit down and allow those who are fathers to come up for a few minutes and share with the congregation their experience of raising their children prior to their incarceration and how they've grown since being here.

I thought that to be a rather considerate gesture by the man of God, if I must say so myself. Although, I knew from the beginning that I had said enough for one morning, I was really looking forward to hearing my brothers share what was in their hearts.

While listening and just enjoying myself, I couldn't help but get a little emotional as some became overwhelmed with tears while trying to find the words to express the harsh reality that they've failed their children. I had hoped that there was something to be said to refute that, but how can you rebut the truth?

Although the judicial system has their share in the blame for the cruel and harsh penalties which usually keep us separated from our children well past adulthood, it was our ignorance that led us into making the thoughtless decision of committing a crime that could potentially destroy our lives and the lives of those whom we love. If nothing else, I pray that the slightest bit of silver lining to this story would be that we channel this sustaining hurt into motivation and inspiration to never, ever make this mistake again, and to teach others to do the same.

I often use my children and our personal situations and circumstances as an example to help encourage others to learn from our mistakes, or even from the good, but I thought it to be only fitting to share an e-mail of my cell mate's daughter, addressed to him. He's been incarcerated going on nineteen years now for a nonviolent offense, and if God doesn't intervene before his release date, which I'm sure He will, he would have done close to thirty years. Here's an example of the effects that this kind of unjust sentence has on a child, even after she's become an adult and married, with children of her own.

SUBJECT: Happy Fathers Day
DATE: 6/19/2011

Hi daddy how are you doing today.... I pray that you are well.. I would like to say that I miss you so much and need you home with me. You are the best daddy that anyone could ever wish for. I know it is father day but for me everyday is father day for me because I pray and wish so bad that you can be home with me.. I hurt so bad and cry so much because I want you home with me. I am 30 years old and still cry for you to be home with me, when you was taken away from me half of me left with you and until you are home with me I will never be complet. I wounder why why why so many times of why God allowed you to be taken from me when the years I needed you the most.. I fell so alone at times and all tied up inside.. I find my self angry at my self and with my husband. I look at my husband and zay and if I feel like he is not spending lots of time with zay I get angry,I feel like father and son is right there together,,when all the time I long for my daddy..I feel like know one understand me like you.. Sometime I just want to understand WHY. Now my brother have been taken from me and his kids..I feel like they are hurting like I have for 18 years. I do not know ?????????? well anyway I love you and know that you will always be the greatest man on earth..I must go for now but remember you always have a child that will always LOVE YOU.I pray that all of my hurt and tears will soon all just STOP... love nicky

What's left to say?

Remembering the Reason for Writing

I just received a letter from my beloved brother, Harold. You remember him. He's the one with cancer and the one whom the Lord used to reveal to me that I was to write this book before going home. We're still waiting on God to manifest his healing and to bring him back here before sending him home to proclaim His goodness and mercy to God's people. But I'm reminded of the words he had spoken to me concerning this book being connected to my release.

Well, I've just passed page 200, and I sense in my spirit that the book itself is prepared and ready to be closed out following my departure from prison. Not only that, but some strange things have been happening lately.

First of all, my account is empty again, and it just so happens that Brother Harold asked me if I could send him some more money. On the same day I received his letter, this young man asked if I wanted to sell my two cooking bowls for sixty dollars. Now I love cooking a little something to eat once a week, and normally I would have said no. But that's a pretty large amount for two inexpensive bowls. Plus, my brother and I could really use the money.

On top of that, within the past week, the young man who was last on suicide watch from Chicago that I've been ministering to needed a pair of headphones; one of the Spanish Christian brothers just came back from court and needed a pair of shoes; another Christian brother just came on the compound and needed a radio.

Well, all these were extra items that I owned; therefore, I gladly gave them away. The ironic thing about that is the fact that this is what a person does when he's about to go home—they give their property away to those to whom they are leaving behind.

Even though this was an afterthought, it was a welcomed one which was well received. I'm fully persuaded that I'm prepared for what awaits me on the outside. May the Lord say the same.

Double Trouble

It's 3:58 a.m., awakened again out of my sleep by a CO: "Malone, you've got suicide duty. I'll be back in about thirty minutes to get you." Besides saying "OK," my first response was, "Shoot! I'm tired of this, devil."

As the CO came back to get me and I began walking across the compound towards medical, I ran into another inmate. He's my relief, the one that they would call in my place in the event that I'm unable to come for some reason. Talk about adding insult to injury. So we're both thinking, how could they have made such a mistake? They could have at least allowed one of us to remain asleep.

As we both walked into medical and walked towards the back where suicide watch is conducted, we noticed that there were two inmates sitting at two separate observation rooms, which means that there were two individuals that were being watched. Never have there been two at one time, at least as long as I've been a suicide companion, and those before me have confirmed this awful truth.

While looking in each room in order to determine which one I felt led to look after, I noticed a familiar face. It was the young man from Chicago that was in here several months ago. I was really stunned due to the fact that I've been spending much time with him on the compound, endeavoring and expecting to see him saved.

The other young man was a Mexican who was not trying to commit suicide. He had other issues going on in his head, which led him to commit various acts that weren't pleasant to the eyes, such as standing up in bed naked doing what appeared to be yoga exercises, urinating on the floor and playing in it, walking in spurts like Tim Conway, and trying to talk with him is like talking to a six-month-old child. You can hardly understand a word he's saying, among other things. So being that I already had a head start with my friend out of Chicago, I decided to begin with him.

I really should have discerned that something was going on with him out of the norm, being that he was in my unit on this past week, too drunk to make it back to his unit. I was disappointed when his drinking buddies came looking for me to tell me that he was asking for me.

They led me to a cell, where he was accompanied by about five other guys trying desperately to sober him up so that his drunken state wouldn't bring heat on their wine-making business.

One thing I don't do is get involved in any way in another man's sin, whether it be helping someone get out of a gambling debt, pay off an alcohol bill, or even helping drunks to sober up someone who's in worse shape than they're in.

But as I considered his need for my help, my love for him, and potentially projecting a picture of God's love to everyone involved who was in need of a savior, although reluctant, I willingly went with them.

One of the guys in the cell said to him, "There's Brother Perry." As he looked up at me, his whole demeanor had changed. He began crying like a baby, and reached for me as though I was his father who had come to rescue him from an abusive babysitter.

As we hugged and he apologized for getting drunk, I walked with him back and forth while ministering to him. Then I relieved him back to those with him to continue their attempt to sober him up. Thankfully he was able to walk back to his unit without falling and undetected.

The next day he saw me and again apologized for his misconduct and then proclaimed that he knew it was my prayers and God's power that brought him safely back to his unit.

Now fast forward. It's days later, and here I am once again talking with him by way of suicide watch. And now I'm learning that his reason for checking in was due to some unfortunate news that he had received which involved him possibly being diagnosed with cancer, accompanied with his wife wanting to leave him over, pardon me for using a legal term, newly discovered evidence concerning his infidelity between him and his wife's friend that took place before coming to prison.

Thankfully this temporary state of depression only lasted a few days. He's now back on the compound, hoping for the best concerning his health condition. Not to mention the fact that his wife heard about him possibly having cancer and desires to remain with him. So now we're left with only one to look after.

It has been a very tedious journey for most of us because most suicide watches rarely last past a week before the individual is either fit to come back on the compound or transferred to another institution suitable to better care for them. In any event, I was given the opportunity to consistently monitor the behavior of this very disturbed young man, even as he monitored mine.

Reading the Word of God, praying, and trying to establish a line of communication with him was routine for me. Ironically, I eventually noticed a change in his mannerisms. There were times when he would start walking up to the door and look through the window to watch me read the Bible, as though he was interested in what I was reading.

At some point I had asked him if he would like for me to read out loud. He slowly nodded his head up and down, as to say, "Yes." So I gladly began reading out loud. After a few minutes, he began walking away as I continued to read out loud, making sure he heard every word.

Less than five minutes later, I heard and felt a pounding and a vibration that was so loud and scary, you would think someone had driven a bulldozer through the wall. It was the guy who was on suicide watch. Apparently the reading of the Word began to agitate the evil spirit or demon within him. So it acted out by pounding on that plexiglas window, harder than any normal man could have, obviously in an attempt to stop me from reading. Mission accomplished.

I have to be honest. I was so frightened at first, and under the illusion that this little frail Mexican demon-possessed man could possibly break this steel or iron door down. With eyes opened as big as a silver dollar, and realizing what had taken place, I immediately began rebuking and taking authority over the demon. I then asked what his name was. The man walked away and said, "Salvador." Almost immediately he went to bed with me left wondering what that demon's name was.

After I had made it back to the unit, I asked a Mexican friend, the one I had sold the two bowls to, if he was familiar with that name and what it meant. He replied, "Yes. It means 'a savior,' or 'a god,' or 'one that makes a sacrifice for the people.'"

I haven't done a follow-up to determine the validity of the meaning that he gave me as of yet; but I'm more disappointed that I was caught off guard and failed to cast the demon out of the man. So you know that I'm eagerly anticipating morning to arrive in order to finish what I had started.

Morning couldn't come fast enough, but it's finally here; and to my surprise, this fellow is doing much better. He spoke to me once he noticed that I was on duty, but he remained asleep throughout my three-hour shift. Not good! Now I'm like an addict who can't get his fix until 4:00 a.m. in the morning.

The next morning arrives, and I'm waiting for him to wake up. Finally he does, but something's surprisingly different about him now. We're talking like two normal human beings. He appears to be in his right mind; the way he walks, all of the insane gestures, none of them seem to be in operation.

So he begins to share with me his concerns, how he wants to talk with his daughter and how his child's mother refuses to allow him based on his past actions and unwarranted deeds that he subjected her to. He went on to talk of how he was once in the church, and how familiar he was with the Scriptures and his problem with some Christians, even pastors, failing to meet God's requirements, to put it nicely. But I continued to listen to him, and he talked so much that I actually looked forward to him tiring himself out and going back to sleep.

After revealing to me all that was in his heart, and after sharing with him the Lord's desire to make him whole in every area of his life, he eventually laid down to try and get some sleep.

While lying down, he said and did something that left me perplexed. He said, "Brother Malone, I hope that the Lord uses you in a great way out there." Then as I responded by confirming that He would, I then told him that the Lord desires to do the same in his life as well. As I made eye contact with him, he gave me a smirk, then pointed his finger at me as though it was a gun, and pulled the trigger. I asked him why he would want to shoot me; he said not a word for the remainder of the session.

The first thing that was mysterious to me was, how did he know my name? Out of all that was said, I don't remember ever telling him my name. The other thing was, after what seemed like a heart-to-heart and intelligent conversation, why would he think of shooting me, then cut off all communication?

Later that day, I concluded that my failing to cast the demon out after he seemingly identified himself to me enabled him to devise a plan that would allow him to remain in his or their place of residence. That plan appeared to be to refrain from manifesting any activities that would reveal their presence. I felt foolish, and now it was time I got bold and took the fight to the enemy.

The very next morning, he didn't even wake up to get his breakfast. One of the guys said he started taking medication that made him sleep. The next morning, no movement whatsoever. That evening I was told that he was taken off of suicide watch and placed into segregation. I can't wait to speak with the psychologist to hopefully inquire as to why that decision was made and whether or not he had a say in the matter.

But when all is said and done, it looks like that was one I let get away. Sorry, my friend. Lesson learned. May the Lord send a laborer across your path that you might be delivered.

Concluding the Matter

Well, I hate to beat a dead horse, but I thought you'd like to know the real reason why the young man was taken off suicide watch and placed in segregation. I was told that he pleaded with the psychologist, insisting to be relocated to that part of the compound and repeatedly proclaimed that he was doing much better. So the doctor told him that the only thing that was lacking concerning his behavior was his endeavor to continue living in a filthy cell. It was said that this guy cleaned the cell so well and so fast from ceiling to floor, one would think that he had a PhD in janitorial services!

An hour or two later he was moved. Now you can say what you want to, but that was one smart, scary devil.

16
The Desire to Be Rich

Thinking on my dear friend Rosie's condition; you know, the fact that she's so limited in what she can or cannot do based on her lack of finances; I can't help but experience a deeper desire to see my deliverance come to pass along with the prosperity that God had confirmed in me.

In considering the pattern that most pastors operate by, I've come to the conclusion that I may have been a bit too hard or critical towards Rosie's pastor. She always raves and speaks very highly of him. Being that she's a woman of great character and discernment, I won't dispute her judgment in this matter. Besides, in years past, he has taken up a love offering a time or two in order to assist her in this lingering debt crisis that she's had to endure.

So I don't believe that the problem is with him, per se, but more so with the method whereby most pastors use in which to teach and to educate their parishioners in developing money management skills, investing, and the beauty of brothers and sisters who are more fortunate, lovingly and liberally sharing and helping the ones who are less fortunate.

While on the subject of finances, I'm reminded of the many prosperity preachers there are in this day and time, attempting to teach their parishioners how to birth or become rich through faith and applying the Word of God, using and standing on Scriptures pertaining to riches; not discerning that they're misapplying and misappropriating God's Word in order to accumulate wealth. Whereas in the end result, the only ones who end up rich are the pastors who receive the countless tithes and offerings from people that have been given a false sense of hope that in their giving through faith leads to prosperity and riches.

This is not a topic that I wish to spend a lot of time on, even though there are countless Scriptures and examples in the Word of God that would confirm this truth. Not only are there examples in the Word, but we can find many in our everyday lives.

For instance, Rosie is a giver and a faithful tither. She believes in the full Gospel, which includes prosperity. But as you know that up until now, she is yet to walk in financial prosperity, or even to receive enough money to cover all of her living expenses on a regular basis.

Now you might say, maybe she's not doing something right. Well, I beg to differ. Maybe it's not God's intention for everyone to be financially rich. And if there was a pattern in which God had established that would mandate riches, maybe it's different from the one that the prosperity preachers and teachers today are presenting.

Let us first visit a few Scriptures concerning the attitude of God towards those who desire to be rich, and hopefully they will interpret themselves.

The book of Proverbs chapter 15 verse 27 says it this way: He that is greedy of gain troubleth his own house. Proverbs chapter 28 verse 20 says that a faithful man shall abound with blessings, but he that maketh haste to be rich shall not be innocent. Verse 22 of that same chapter says that he that hasteth to be rich hath an evil eye, and considereth not that poverty shall come upon him.

First Timothy chapter 6 beginning in at verse 6 through verse 10 says it this way: [6]But godliness with contentment is great gain. [7]For we brought nothing into this world, and it is certain we can carry nothing out. [8]And having food and raiment let us be there with content. [9]But they that will be rich fall into temptation and a snare, and into many foolish and hurtful lusts, which drown men in destruction and perdition. [10]For the love of money is the root of all evil; which while some coveted after, they have erred from the faith, and pierced themselves through with many sorrows (KJV).

There are so many more, but for the sake of time, I believe you get my point, or rather, God's point.

Now, is God against those who are rich, or is He responsible for making some rich? Of course He's not against the rich; and yes, He has made some rich. But God also has a profile in which He goes by or a standard that one must meet in order to receive riches from Him. One of those requirements is that a person doesn't pursue riches; another is that he walks in humility; and the third is that he or she fears the Lord.

Proverbs chapter 22 and verse 4 is one of many Scriptures that dictates this truth. It says that by humility and fear of the Lord are riches, and honour, and life. The word "riches" in this particular Scripture means "wealth," "far richer," or "accumulation."

Sometimes we tend to take Scriptures out of context. For instance, when a Scripture is really not talking about monetary or material things in order to prove our point, we'll take a Scripture that's talking about prosperity in a spiritual sense only and relate it to finance. Now to put a face, or rather, faces, to some men that met God's standard of being blessed with riches, there's Job, Abraham, Solomon, and David, just to name a few.

Without going into extensive details of the life that these men lived prior to and during the time that they had come into their wealth, I encourage you to study and determine for yourselves whether or not those men fit the profile.

Another key element that I failed to mention which is equally important in obtaining riches from the Lord is one's ability to steward over or successfully manage such a responsibility. Jesus demonstrated this truth in the book of Matthew chapter 25, beginning at verse 14 through 29. Although He was referring to the Kingdom of God, He used a monetary illustration, which included man's ability, in order to make His point.

There's nothing wrong with wanting to do well in life and store up something for your children and grandchildren. God encourages that. But when we pursue riches, we are in error, according to the Word of God.

Is Anyone Prepared to Die?

In speaking with one of my aunts just a few days ago, I asked a question that's very common for men in prison to ask their loved ones: How is everyone doing? She began by individually detailing certain health concerns within the family before exhaustion sat in, and out of what sounded like discouragement, took a shortcut and stated that everyone was sick in one way or the other.

I'm aware that many of my relatives are beyond the age of fifty, but I'm also aware that hardly anyone has surrendered their lives to the Lord. Which means that no one is ready to die, because no good thing awaits anyone beyond the grave who has not prepared themselves for eternity. God forbid, but to witness the loss of a loved one who has failed to make peace with the Lord would grieve me greatly and add insult to injury, knowing that we won't be together in the life to come.

Today is September the 26th, which marks the thirteenth anniversary date of my incarceration. In the Bible, Jacob's son, Joseph, was sold into slavery by his brothers, where he remained for thirteen years until God's Word came to pass concerning him; whereas he was not only used to save the lives of his family, but the lives of everyone else as well.

Joseph's family is no different from mine; they both need to experience God's grace and mercy. The Lord did it for them; surely He can do the same for mine. There is no respect of persons with God. Likewise, just as He used Joseph to bring about this miraculous deliverance that had blessed many, I have no doubt that He can and will do the same through me.

Joseph was a great man of God. The only difference between him and me is that he's in heaven and I'm on my way. As always, I look to be going home at any moment, and to see the salvation of the Lord being manifested in the lives of my family, as well as many others. To God be the glory.

Testimonies

Today is November the 3rd, and I'm a papa again. My youngest daughter, Kiara, just gave birth to a cute little baby boy. His name is Kayden. I believe that makes number six for me. Oh well, there's definitely no need for me to consider having any more children of my own. Four children and six grands will do. But I'm so blessed to be given the privilege of loving them all unconditionally, and to impart something in them that has been imparted in me: God's Word.

The Bible tells us that it has everything in it that pertains to life and Godliness. Children are always a testimony to the goodness of God. Psalm 127 says that children are an heritage of the Lord: and the fruit of the womb is his reward. It also says that happy or blessed is the man that hath his quiver full of them; I am.

While speaking on the goodness of God, there's another testimony I'd like to share with you that has also blessed me tremendously. It was about two weeks ago I had spoken to my sister over the phone, and as always, she greeted me by saying, "What's up, gal?" As you know, she's been joking with me in this manner for over twenty years now; and even though I resent it, especially as a man of God, what am I to do other than expressing that fact to her and keeping her in prayer?

As we went further into the conversation, she continued to use other language that really grieved my spirit. Of course this has happened many times; I mean it's no secret, although she's a good person in her own way. Still, she's always been a strong, tough, and mean individual in some ways as well. But she is a loving person. It's just a tough kind of love. That's all she knows.

Anyway, this was a time when the Holy Spirit had spoken expressly to me in saying, "It's time to use the authority that I have given you to put an end to the grieving of my Spirit." I could hardly sleep that night, anticipating daybreak in order to begin writing what would be a challenging letter once my cellie had gone to work.

There were only three things that I wanted to try and make known to my sister: that I loved her; that I was no longer her brother of old, but a true man of God; and the need to redefine the way that we conduct our conversations. Although it wasn't written exactly in those words; however, it was written in the spirit of love, giving her the liberty to accept or reject this very necessary change, and believing that God would perform and fulfill in her heart the reality of who He has made and ordained me to be: a minister of righteousness.

Anyway, after writing her and with much prayer, it was time to call to see how things were going. She answered the phone, and for the first time in over twenty years, she neglected to address me in a derogatory way. She said, "Hello there"; and although I sensed the restraint it took for her to keep from using a phrase that had become as natural to her as calling on the name of the Lord is to me, I was grateful to God for what He had done through my letter.

We didn't talk about the letter. You know my sister; that's not her style. Unfortunately, she wasn't feeling very well. Surprisingly to her as well as myself, I asked if I could pray for her over the phone. She responded by saying I could. By the time I had stopped praying, my sister was unable to talk from being overwhelmed with tears—the first time ever I've witnessed my sister in this condition.

I was left with mixed emotions. A part of me was in awe of what God was doing in these brief moments on the phone, while another part of me was in sorrow over the emotional state of my sister. I kept calling her name, anticipating her to say something, but all I heard was the voice of my mother saying, "Hello, my son." My sister had given her the phone due to her temporary inability to speak.

My mother and I refused to even comment on what had just taken place. We just continued to talk as though nothing ever happened. But we both knew that something did. God showed up, and had begun something that I'm believing will lead to the saving of my sister; and not only her, but my entire family. And that is, the unveiling of an authentic transformation had taken place in the life of one of their own; and the possibility of jailhouse religion would be dismissed.

The last testimony is that I've just received an e-mail from my second oldest daughter, named Salena. She wanted me to know that she had just graduated from college, and that she would be walking across the stage in a couple of months to get her degree. I am so proud of my baby. It is such a blessing to know that my children didn't do too badly while I've been away.

You probably don't remember Salena. I don't talk about her much, but God knows I love her just as I love my other children. We didn't have a close relationship while I was out there, due to negative influences that I allowed to help dictate the choices that I made in life. But there's no one to blame but me. Nevertheless, I've purposed in my heart to devote much quality time into building the kind of father-daughter relationship that my little princess deserves.

She is such a beautiful and ambitious young lady, and I'm so proud of her.

11-11-11 / Remembering a Vet

Today is November 11, 2011, Veteran's Day. I'm reminded of my grandfather, who passed away this year. He was a veteran who fought in World War II. Since his passing, there has been a reoccurring moment of regret concerning my last contact with him.

It was my last phone call to the hospital, days before his death. My aunt the evangelist was there, and I asked her to put the phone to my daddy's ear. I wanted to pray for him, and to thank him for an awesome job he did in raising me, and to let him know how much I loved him.

Unfortunately, there was a bit of confusion on my part. All I heard was the evangelist constantly talking so loud and clear that I assumed she was still on the phone. So I kept calling her name but got no response, not knowing that my grandfather, who was unable to talk, was on the phone the whole while.

After about a minute or so had passed, my aunt had stopped doing what she's good at, which is talking, and noticed that my granddaddy had been trying desperately to get her attention. So she took the phone from his ear and told him that he couldn't be getting all excited like that. So I'm thinking, *You can't shut your mouth for a minute and monitor Daddy while I say a few words to him?*

Anyway, I told her that he was trying to get her attention and she said that she knew. For me, that was a missed opportunity that I can never get back; one that I believe would have meant the world to my daddy, even while he was on his deathbed.

That's a memory I'm looking forward to putting behind me. But I honor you on today, Daddy, for your service to your country, and most importantly, for choosing to serve as a loving father, and to have made such an impact in my life. Love you.

Merry Christmas 2011

Today is December 25th, 2011. It's Christmas, and even though I'm still in prison, it has been a wonderful day for me thus far. This morning we had a beautiful program in church. There were about six brothers selected to give a presentation on the various mindsets or perspectives on how Christmas is perceived. There was Satan's view, commercialization, the world, parents, religions, and finally, God's view.

I was selected to speak on the world's view, but once it was over with, I believe that everyone left with a balanced and accurate assessment on the true meaning of Christmas.

I'm sure that some of my readers have determined in their hearts not to acknowledge or celebrate Christmas, mainly due to a major distortion of it that has been proclaimed by Satan in his attempt to use people, the media, money, etc., for the sole purpose of silencing the cry of a little baby by the name of JESUS, who came into this world to save it from sin and from the wrath to come; to reunite it, or rather, us, back to a loving God.

Christmas is not about a tree, lights, presents, and all of the other perishable things in which we relate to Christmas. These things aren't necessarily bad in themselves, but we mustn't allow them to cover up the true meaning of Christmas.

I'm not going to give a history lesson or some educated writing on the origin of Christmas, but I just believe that the majority of us do believe that Jesus the Christ was born one day. Now it may not have been in the month of December, or even on the twenty-fifth of any month. But we as Christians are celebrating the reality that this Jesus was born one day, and that is where our hope lies.

So please, let's not continue to wrestle with this issue. Let's try and love one another and respect the others' convictions. After all, that is what this day represents: God loving us so much, that He gave us Jesus. What a gift!

Speaking of gifts, I spoke with my son on today. You remember his encounter with the law that I shared with you some time ago. I was told that he was arrested for drugs and for carrying an illegal weapon. Well, it turns out that it wasn't for drugs. Instead it was for two separate gun charges. However, he decided to join the National Guard, and they assisted in helping him to stay out of prison. So to know that my boy will be there when I come home and won't have to see the inside of a prison is truly a gift from the Lord. Apart from this day being represented as my Savior's birth, this awesome news gave me more of a reason to have a Merry Christmas.

In light of that, I've decided to end part one of this two-part book in order to get it out on the bookshelves as soon as possible as my gift to you. It is my prayer that you will not only enjoy every word of this book, but that you will be enlightened, that you will grow and mature in this thing called life, and that you will become engaged and get involved in this project. You are special to God and to me. MERRY CHRISTMAS!

I'll talk with you soon in part 2.

                          Sincerely,
                          Perry

More About the Project

This project will be fully staffed with the following positions being filled by reputable and well-experienced individuals, in order to insure that our interests will be properly and aggressively pursued and obtained.

- Business and Legal Attorney of forty-plus years of experience
- Head supervisor and business manager with over twenty-five years of experience
- Civil rights representative and lobbyist with over thirty-five years of experience
- Press rep with many years of experience

The goal is not only to force Congress to bring back parole as well as the changing of other laws with the ultimatum of the millions of HIGOP members which will be confirmed via website, that they are registered voters who are prepared to come out in record numbers to vote them out if their interests are not adhered to; but it is also geared towards going into the prisons with the goal of helping to aspire and empower the men and women in becoming better fathers and mothers, husbands and wives, as well as successful and productive leaders in their communities.

We are endeavoring to begin creating businesses that would afford the multitude of men and women that will be exiting prison an opportunity to not only have a job, but the potential of it leading to a career; even to the extent of owning their own business.

This project is expected to be nationally televised, as well as being heard on many nationally syndicated radio shows. These are just a few things that you can expect to come to fruition in the near future. There's more to come, and you'll be the first to hear of the many endeavors in which we're expected to accomplish.

Sincerely,
H I G O P Project Manager

Attention Reader

We are excited about introducing to you what we believe to be one of the most meaningful books you'll ever read. This book is the beginning of a project with a divine purpose to help turn the hearts of the fathers back to the children, to advocate for the victims of injustice, and uniting their voices to speak in the ears of lawmakers.

ENOUGH IS ENOUGH. To help create a sound and functional household for the underprivileged surrounding neighborhoods that would instill in them a desire to climb to higher heights; even to the extent of becoming entrepreneurs, and enabling them to do so.

This book is part one of a memoir that illustrates many true and personal life experiences, such as government corruption, injustice, dysfunctional families, sexual intercourse, the love of money, parenting, government informants, and much more, based on how they're viewed through the mind of God as well as man. All to help stabilize the family and structuring it the way God intended for it to be.

In the recent past, a study found that there were about 2.3 million people incarcerated here in the United States, which is more than any other country, with 140,610 serving a life sentence and two-thirds of them being black and Latino. Nearly one-third of the total number of inmates serving life has no possibility for parole, and sadly, many of which are nonviolent offenders. Surely we must demand change.

Join us, and become a full supporter and member of this monumental project, beginning with purchasing this book to help finance this worthy cause. The very future of our children pleads for your assistance.

Enclosed you will find the information on how to purchase this book, as well as how loved ones of the incarcerated, including those who are willing to stand for a cause greater than themselves, can join this project.

We are especially welcoming those who are of voting age, so that the ones who will be lobbying for and with you will have a much greater tool of influence to take with them in their request for change, beginning with reinstituting a parole system for the incarcerated that would afford those who have demonstrated a genuine change.

We also welcome financial contributions to this worthy cause from those who are able and led to do so. Lastly, we welcome you into the HIGOP family, and look forward to change in the near future.

I wish above all things that thou mayest prosper and be in health, even as thy soul prospereth (3 John 2).

To become a member of H I G O P LLC., you can go online to register at facebook.com/higoppm or send a $10 annual membership fee along with your contact information to H I G O P LLC., P.O. Box 66557, Mobile, AL 36606.

If this book has been a blessing to you and you'd like to share your thoughts with the author, you can write to me or email me.

Author's Contact Information
Perry Malone 07143-003
Federal Correctional Institution
2680 Hwy. 301 South
Jesup, GA 31599
Email address: higoppm@yahoo.com